MISSISSIPPI R.
IOWA
Tama
Williamsburg
North English
Sigourney
ILLINOIS
La Plata
Moberly
Jefferson City
Alma
Eskridge
Council Grove
Olpe
Climax
MISSOURI
Salem
Cape Girardeau
Cairo
Golconda
Shawneetown
Cave-in Rock
New Harmony
Mt. Vernon
Henderson
Owensboro
Brandenburg
KENTUCKY
WABASH R.
INDIANA
OHIO R.
Maysville
Vanceburg
Gallipolis
OHIO
Portsmouth
Marietta
Mt. Morris
Hundred
WEST VIRGINIA
PENNSYLVANIA
Bedford
Bedford Springs
Gettysburg
Lancaster
Allentown
Bordentown
Atlantic Highlands
NEW JERSEY
Imslaytown
Atlantic Ocean
MISSISSIPPI R.
Gulf of Mexico
map by palacios

THE LOST
TOWNS AND ROADS
OF AMERICA

# THE LOST
# TOWNS AND ROADS
# OF AMERICA

*J. R. Humphreys*

PHOTOGRAPHS BY THE AUTHOR

*Doubleday & Company, Inc.    Garden City, New York*

*1961*

*for Peggy*

# CONTENTS

*Contents*

## Contents

# JOURNEYING
## INTO THE PAST

*New and old maps. The timeless towns of the
Thirteen Colonies, New England, the South, the
Northwest, the Southwest, the Middle West.*

The whole face of America has changed from what it used
to be when I was a kid and I find I've had to adjust my vision
to see it as it is. The automobiles and the highways make the
difference because the changes are along those highways and
along the streets in the cities that become highways at their
outskirts. Along the turnpikes and freeways, villages and
hamlets and metropolitan suburbs are joining to form the
promised "strip" cities of the future—one of which is expected to stretch, within the next twenty years, from the
Atlantic Ocean to the Mississippi River. At the same time,
something verging on fantasy is happening in America.

Because of this changing topography, I think it is possible
to pick roads to follow across the country, from the Atlantic to
the Pacific, that could make a Rip Van Winkle who has slum-
bered twenty-five, fifty, even a hundred years, think the whole
nation still looks pretty much as it should.

Following such carefully selected roads, a view of the land from coast to coast can be gained that hasn't been seen in a long, long time by motorists. It can be, virtually, a trip into and then across a countryside buried in the past but far from dead; not just a journey from ghost town to ghost town, but a journey as though by time machine from one living American Brigadoon to another.

The turnpikes and freeways and the larger of the highways would have to be avoided; for these are the main streets not of a town or of a city but of a nation, and it's up these main streets that Time is moving so swiftly with alteration and change.

For some time I've been carrying in my mind a picture of America with little lines crinkling out from the big highways, wrinkling across a rural countryside through small towns seldom visited any more—just because of the highways—and these are to me the "lost" roads of an older America.

I think I first put thought to these "lost" roads around the tail end of the Depression, back about the time the East Belt Line was built past my grandmother's house on the outskirts of Grand Rapids, Michigan. After that Belt Line bypass was completed, it took so long for traffic to discover the clean concrete pathway to the northern hills and lakes that I began to think of it as a road the highway department had built and lost.

I had a couple of tennis rackets, one of them a bottle-shaped antique that belonged to my Uncle Allen; and whenever I could hunt up a partner, we'd go out on the vacant highway and stretch a rope across it for a net. Then we'd stand back, and using the big sections of the new pavement for our courts, we'd have a game of tennis. The road stayed unfound all summer. It was a rare game a passing car interrupted.

In time, of course, the road ceased to be lost. When I returned to my grandmother's the following summer, I was told to keep off the highway. Traffic was a good deal heavier—and it got more so year by year.

As year followed year after the Depression, and as the traffic on the big new highways all over the country increased, it was a different sort of road that became lost. Though I don't mean "lost" so much as I do forgotten or abandoned.

New highways, slicing across the country, across once inviolable farmland, cut off a lot of old roads and isolated a lot of towns. And as the towns became isolated, rincons of timelessness settled about them. They rarely perished. Caught and held in place, time flowed up, then around and past them.

Timeless towns and whole areas of the past must lie along those old roads, I figured. New Jersey is, in many places, deep in Colonial and Revolutionary times, and there would be roads that went through those areas. In Pennsylvania, the Amish still live on as they've lived, with little change, for a couple of hundred years. Beyond Pennsylvania, there is the whole of the Ohio River that I thought I'd like to follow— through river port towns that had in all probability remained unchanged since the river-boat days because the rivers—the "roads that moved"—once the main highways of America, had been abandoned by the big passenger boats.

Across the Mississippi is a land of Middle Western small towns and of farmland that had not, I hoped, changed much in the last half century; and beyond the rich shore of the prairie and on into the Southwest lies a land where Spanish and the languages of the American Indian are still spoken on the streets and in adobe houses. Beyond that and westward are the open skies, mountains, rangeland, little of it settled

15

with houses even now; the Mormons of Utah; and finally, the shores of California.

We decided, Mrs. H. and I, to make the trip and see what it looked like for ourselves; we decided to make a trip into time.

Because we'd be visiting small towns that had been cut off, much as Mark Twain describes the Mississippi's manner of cutting off towns from the river's commerce, I knew the maps passed out at gasoline stations would serve us for the trip. "These cut-offs," says Twain, "have had curious effects: they have thrown several river towns out into rural districts, and built up sand bars and forests in front of them. The town of Delta used to be three miles below Vicksburg: a recent cut-off has radically changed the position, and Delta is now two miles above Vicksburg.

"Both of these river towns have been retired to the country by that cut-off . . ."

It's not hard to find innumerable towns dotted along the little dark loops cut off by the red lines of the highways on all our standard state maps that fit the same description.

For the detailed designs of the roads too small to make the state maps, I thought I'd run down the individual road charts of the counties through which we'd pass on our way west.

In the New York Public Library at Fifth Avenue and 42nd Street, there's a map room which has the general shape of a shoebox. Maps from all over the country and the world are filed on shelves that run from floor to ceiling. Two long strips of fluorescent lights shine down and three high windows, facing to the west, let in light across the edge of buildings that seem old enough to place one roughly in antiquity.

In the wall opposite the entrance, there's a solid bank of

catalogue cards. I'd pulled out the file on New Jersey and was looking it over when one of the librarians came over and asked if he could be of any help.

When I told him what I was up to, that I wanted a map of every county through which I'd pass on the way to California, he shook his head. They not only didn't have maps on every county in the country, but there were counties, he said, that had never been surveyed. These were largely in the South and the Southwest, the unmapped areas; and so I went to work, with his help, on what was available.

I noticed, going through the cards, that the county maps on tap dated, for the most part, back to the days of World War I, when so many of our county roads were mapped for Rural Free Delivery service. This was good enough for my purpose since few of the roads would have changed; but copyrights (a copyright is good for twenty-eight years, and it can be renewed for another twenty-eight) stopped me from having photostats made of most of them.

That's how I came to acquire a map of Greene County, Pennsylvania, published in 1865. That old Greene County map—I sat staring at it. A dozen or more of the little towns around the county were drawn with the grids of their streets around the map's borders: Mount Morris in Perry Township and Rices Landing in Jefferson Township. The buildings along the streets were blocked in with the names of the people who lived there beside them. And up in one corner was a picture of McConnell, the man who'd made the map. He'd even marked all the farms along the county roads with dots and put in the names of the farmers. And I kept thinking: It's here in my hands—whole fields of the past, unchanged. It began to seem to me that I had an actual map to the past with maybe everything on that map still as it was ninety-five years ago.

It's easy, with an old map in your hands, for a mood like that to roll around you with ethereal smoke and timeless haze. Maps, printed maps at least, date back to the fifteenth century when they were printed from woodcuts and copper plates . . . but maps, as such, are as old as some of our earliest records of civilization. There are clay tablets in the British Museum which represent land surveys made earlier than 2000 B.C., one of which outlines lower Babylonia.

On early maps, the ocean surrounded the known world; it circled it like a river; and some of those maps located Paradise. It was up at the top of the world in a land known as the Far East. Maps weren't entirely accurate in those days either. Many a year later, Christopher Columbus, guided along by Paolo dal Pazzo Toscanelli's mapwork, figured for sure he'd swung his ships up along the shores of Asia. The Orientals on shore had to be Indians. His maps indicated this was India; they'd be citizens of India, that was all! Today, there are still occasional travelers with a map in their hands as confounded as any explorer in the Middle Ages. A map is still a challenge and an adventure, but the old maps carry a whiff of magic as well. The map of Greene County had the breath and air and climate of the last century hovering over it and around my shoulders.

And so did some of the other old maps I saw. There was a map that George Washington had drawn of the land around Greene County in the 1750s. But in those days the county was only some land that lay in the Colony of Virginia. A map from that period used on the London Reprint of Washington's

"Journal to the Ohio," 1754, gave me a look at territory we'd be passing through when the Alleghenies were known as the Endless Mountains and the Ohio as the Fair River. A later map, showing now the roads as well as the rivers, confined itself to Ohio, Illinois, and Indiana. It was published in 1835 and along the Ohio River, the towns of Marietta, Gallipolis, Cincinnati, Madison, and Shawneetown had appeared. That map carried with it the charge of the past. All the old maps did and I felt it, as I looked them all over one by one.

The public libraries are not the only sources of old maps. Every state and county historical society also has them. Perhaps the largest collection is located with the Library of Congress.

The business of publishing atlases got its start in the eighteenth century, between 1790 and 1795, though county atlases didn't get moving until the late 1830s. Between 1893 and 1923, George A. Ogle and Co. of Chicago published some five hundred county atlases. Few of these are now available; but there is at least one outfit that specializes in old maps, and that's Argosy Book Stores, Inc., at 114 East 59th Street, New York City. Their prices range upward from $2 for a map one hundred years old; some go for as high as $100. Fifteen dollars is more the average price. They handle mail order requests. If you tell them the state and even the county you want, they'll try to find the map.

Advertising for old maps in small-town papers, as well as hunting around in your own and your relatives' attics, will turn up items as old and quaint as Mendenhall's Guide and Road Map of Ohio, which described the road conditions between cities. "OTTAWA TO WAUSEON—North, passing 1 mile east of Holgate 16 fair, clay; to Napoleon 26, good, gravel, level; Wauseon 37, good, gravel, some hills."

For up-to-date county road maps, it's best to write directly to the county, or to drop in at the courthouse when you're driving through the county seat. The map for Lancaster County, Pennsylvania, was sent to me without charge, but maps of other counties around the country I found to range from twenty-five cents to a dollar.

State Highway Departments have a good supply of county maps. The New Mexico State Highway Department, which I imagine is typical of other states, sold maps for all its counties. The price: $1.00 each. They also sold quadrangle maps which divided the state into 127 pieces for forty cents apiece. One of New Mexico's most interesting maps for our trip was free. This was the map indicating the state's traffic flow for all roads bearing U.S. and state numerals. It was useful in locating the least-traveled roads, and so what would probably be the best-preserved countryside.

It's also possible to buy quadrangle maps for any of our 50 states from International Map Co. Inc., 140 Liberty St., New York, 38, New York.

As for cities, Geographia Map Company, Inc., of 256 East 49th Street, New York 17, New York, has street guides for fifty-three cities in the United States, Canada, and England—or how to avoid progressive, downtown areas in our major cities.

But our stand-by, our crutch, our sometimes vague guide for at least 95 per cent of the trip was the state map found on the racks in gas stations across the country.

Most timeless towns, like gold or fantasy, are where you find them. There isn't any specific guide or map to follow that will lead you from one to another. There are only a few general reference books that help. You drive along following leads and hunches (*a stone, a leaf, an unfound door*) and then, around the next bend in the road, a town comes up that looks as if no eyes had seen it in fifty or a hundred years.

Found doors and found towns have the appearance of being both often found and often gazed upon. They know they're attractive, and they're proud of their timelessness. The unfound towns, on the other hand, are usually unconscious of their charm and include, among their citizens, those who are touchy about being behind the times. Then there are the timeless towns that have been re-created, like Williamsburg, Virginia, that aren't so much to be discovered by the time-traveler as they are themselves travelers in time. Williamsburg seems to have been sent, intact, into the future—into our own present, that is—and its houses have the new look of recently built homes. So there are three kinds of lost or timeless towns: the found, the unfound, and the re-created. All have something to recommend them, but the unfound you have to find for yourself; and it was the out-of-the-way and undiscovered towns with the face of an earlier era in which we were mostly interested on this trip.

The history and the fiction we'd already read (or wanted to read) provided leads; and by history, I especially include the local history on the shelves of small-town libraries. The series of books on the rivers of America was valuable because so many of the oldest towns were built along the banks of waterways that provided power as well as transportation.

But the reference books we used most were the state guides and AAA tour books. During the last Depression, the Work Projects Administration put gangs of unemployed writers to work on projects that resulted in our various state guides. Even the smallest libraries seem to have at least a regional selection of these books.

The book on Maine, one of the American Guide Series, with an introductory letter by Harry L. Hopkins, the administrator, sets forth the general background of that state, describes its cities and towns and then suggests tours along its many roads with mile-by-mile descriptions. It's typical of all the other state guides.

The AAA tour books, covering the United States not only by state but by whole regions at a swipe, also describe cities and towns and places of interest—and along the way recommend places to eat and to stop for the night. In addition, they describe the accommodations and list rates.

Both of these reference sources, however, pass over the largest part of the small lost or unfound timeless towns, and many an atmospheric restaurant with excellent food sits unknown to all but the local folks, because it's a little too far off the main car trails. So you have to begin with general references and then hunt around along the small roads and see what turns up.

We missed, of course, a lot of interesting towns that way. You don't know what's across the next hill, but what's more frustrating, you often come to forks and don't know which to take. Whichever you take, you'll miss what was down the other branch. And was it, James T. Jackson wonders, "out of a similar moment of indecision that many of us owe our present manner of speech, as well as our present religious denomination . . . to some day in 1830, perhaps, when it looked muddy on the trail north, and muddy on the trail south, and some great-great-grandfather spun a coin, and took one route before the other, for good and all?"

You come to a fork and you have to decide, because the towns along the way aren't all as alike as peas in a pod, whatever you've heard. Things will look different; and when we took one branch instead of another, as we crossed the country, it was, I regret, for good and all.

In deciding on our particular route, in fact, there were whole areas of the country we had to pass up. The five major areas, or regions, I want some day to explore by car, I count as the territory of the Thirteen Colonies, the South, the Middle West, the Southwest, and the Northwest. I don't think I'll try to define their limits. That's one thing about our boundaries: they're not very neat or precise, and a man can argue his head hollow putting a boundary around, say, the South.

The original Thirteen Colonies break down into four New England states, New York, New Jersey, Pennsylvania, Maryland, Delaware, and four Southern states. But even such regional breakdowns are rough, and within the vague divisions come vague subdivisions.

However, one of these days, I will make a separate trip out of New England. I want to save New England for some fall. I'll pass through many of the found, timeless towns of Connecticut, even though I've already seen most of them, and I'll head for the top of Vermont and New Hampshire and for Maine. Up there, I think, are many undiscovered timeless towns.

Maine, larger than Vermont, New Hampshire, and Rhode Island put together, is a wooded, mountainous state with better than 5000 rivers and streams—and though long devoid of its earliest inhabitants, the Red Paint People, it still has some pristinely primitive and barely explored areas. I would like to drive through those areas and I'd like to drive along Maine's coast.

In the northern part of Vermont and New Hampshire, I'd like to take a look around Lake Champlain, the Green Mountains, Newport on Lake Memphremagog, and the lakes in the northeast corner of Vermont. The White Mountains in northern New Hampshire look promising and so does all that forest and farmland north of the Connecticut Lakes. It must still be pretty wild because it wasn't so long ago there was a bounty on bears in the northern part of New Hampshire.

Among the Vermont towns I'd want to take a look at for their timelessness are Burlington, Greensboro, Morgan Center, Lyndonville, Peacham, Lower Waterford, and Craftsbury. And in New Hampshire, Newport, for just one place, is somewhere I'd head. Along the way, I'd expect a lot of old inns, some that I've heard about like Elkins Tavern between Danville and Groton.

I'd go in the fall when the countryside is in full color and the bulletin boards in the post offices and the local newspapers are announcing Grange suppers and festivals, and we could pick up tickets to huge spreads of baked Vermont ham, puff-topped shepherd's pie, crushed baked beans, and freshly pressed cider.

Another region I am saving is the South. But it wouldn't be a winter trip.

I like the way W. J. Cash described the South, and he was hardly a booster of the regional chauvinist variety. "The country is one of extravagant colors, of proliferating foliage and bloom, of flooding yellow sunlight, and above all perhaps, of haze. Pale blue fogs hang above the valleys in the morning, the atmosphere smokes faintly at midday, and through the long slow afternoon, cloud-stacks tower from the horizon and the earth-heat quivers upward through the iridescent air, blurring every outline and rendering every object vague and problematical. I know that winter comes to the land, certainly. I know there are days when the color and the haze are stripped away and the real stands up in drab and depressing harshness. But these things pass and are forgotten.

"The dominant mood, the mood that lingers in the memory, is one of well-nigh drunken reverie—of a hush that seems all the deeper for the far-away mourning of the hounds and the far-away crying of the doves—of such sweet and inexorable opiates as the rich odors of hot earth and pinewood and the perfume of the magnolia in bloom—of soft languor creeping through the blood and mounting surely to the brain . . . It is a mood, in sum, in which direct thinking is all but impossible, a mood in which the mind yields almost perforce to drift and in which the imagination holds unchecked sway, a mood in which nothing any more seems improbable save the puny inadequateness of fact, nothing incredible save the bareness of truth . . ." It was in such an atmosphere, says Cash, that the romantic South of plantation days reared itself.

In spite of the change in the last twenty years, a great deal still remains of its old and even of its mythopoetic character. There are still collard patches, and restaurants serve turnip greens if you want to go so far as a side dish of spring sass. Mobile's gone big and industrial, but when the azaleas are in bloom early in the spring of the year, the twenty-mile drive through the azaleas goes by some impressive old homes that carry you back. James Street's favorite all-Southern Deep

South city was Memphis, Tennessee. "It's not," he says, "that the South remembers the Civil War, but, rather that we can't forget it. It frowns at us from a thousand courthouse monuments and haunts us from a hundred thousand tombstones. It speaks to us from hotels named for our generals, from highways named for our heroes."

The population of the South was always thinly spread about; there weren't a lot of towns. But there are a number that date back to the plantation days and a few that date back long before that, even.

I'd like to roll South down along the Mississippi, through Memphis and then Greenville and Vicksburg and Natchez, Mississippi. Then I'd cut across Louisiana to Lafayette. In the southern part of Louisiana, below the Red River, there are still buggies driving about, and there's a French atmosphere. I've heard Lafayette has some of it. And beside the Red River, in "old" Louisiana, is Natchitoches, one of our oldest settlements, with many of its old buildings still along the streets. Near Lafayette, from Donaldsonville to Golden Meadows, I'd want to drive that hundred-mile stretch along Bayou La Fourche with its old houses I've heard so much about. I'd drive the river road between Baton Rouge and New Orleans. I'd look about in New Orleans too.

There's a lot to see in the South. On the Atlantic Coast, there's Charleston and Savannah. They're drenched in time. Once, in Knoxville, Tennessee, I spent a night in the President Polk Room in the Maxwell House. It was like sleeping in the elegance of the long ago. The same kind of rooms are to be found in Williamsburg.

Returning north from New Orleans, I'd cut up toward the Great Smoky Mountains and the Shenandoah Valley and

# LOST ROADS

...are those emptied of their old traffic...

PENNSYLVANIA TURNPIKE

. . . by the long four-lane expressways.

There are abandoned roads that seem to lead all the way back to the beginning.

NEAR MOUNT MORRIS, PENNSYLVANIA

Like all roads, they begin small.

OLD COACH ROAD ALONG ROUTE 120, SIERRA NEVADA MOUNTAINS,
CALIFORNIA

GREENE COUNTY, PENNSYLVANIA

They begin as driveways.

They come out of woods.

STIVER PARK, PENNSYLVANIA

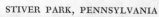

They cross streams where gold can still be panned.

THE RIO DE LAS ANIMAS PERDIDAS, NEAR DURANGO, COLORADO

WEST OF MONTROSE, COLORADO ON ROUTE 90

Lost roads move across a timeless countryside.

They pass homemade signs instead of billboards.

EAST OF TRENTON, NEW JERSEY

ALCALDE, NEW MEXICO

They move up timeless streets . . .

. . . past timeless doors.

TIERRA AMARILLA, NEW MEXICO

DELAWARE RIVER AND CANAL, ROUTE 32, NEAR LUMBERVILLE, PENNSYLVANIA
Like rivers, they widen as they join and they flow to the sea.

along the way I'd take in the sight of things again at Andrew Jackson's old home, the Hermitage; and I'd stop off at Lexington, Virginia, to see if the gate of the past still hangs unhooked in that town. And I'd drop by the grave of a hero of mine, and a lot of other northerners, Stonewall Jackson. I'd certainly want to see Washington's house again at Mount Vernon.

Beyond the Mississippi River, I would head for the Northwest, that land at the end of the Oregon Trail. With just a few leads to follow, as I had for New England and the South, I think I'd run into enough of the unfound kind of timeless towns.

Around Walla Walla, Washington, I'd follow the roads laid down over the old Colville Wagon Trail, cut into the earth north of the Snake River when that country was opened for settlement in 1858. Delaney was an early boom town in that area, and I've heard that northwest of Delaney, on the Snake, the old Lyons Cable-Ferry is still in use. It's nearly a hundred years old and still runs in much the same manner it always has, for just about the same fare, which is around a dollar a crossing.

Up in the corner of Washington, near Seattle, I'd like to go by ferry and side roads to Port Townsend which hasn't changed much in the last seventy years, and I'd like to see, in the same area, Poulsbo, sometimes known as Little Norway.

In Oregon, I've heard of Jacksonville on Route 238. It's an old gold-mining town, but not a ghost town. The old West Side Territorial Road to Monroe from Anlaut looks promising.

But we were going to miss a lot. We were missing out on Weed, California, and California's Route 49 that runs through so many old mining towns. We were missing out on little roads I've driven in Colorado like the Sunshine Canyon

Road out of Boulder that runs to Estes Park through Gold Hill and Ward—a graveled pathway through the old days for an automobile.

We wouldn't be seeing the Navajo lands in Arizona and New Mexico around Window Rock and Canyon de Chelly, with the Navajos driving horse-drawn wagons and herding sheep, all in tribal dress.

We weren't to see Jackson Hole in Wyoming, and all of Montana and the Dakotas, though they have their timeless towns too, as well as their landscape that time doesn't seem to touch. There aren't many narrow-gauge tracks and trains still running, but in the Black Hills, through five miles of wild countryside, the Black Hills Central Railroad still makes trips and carries passengers. I'm saving for another day Nebraska, that lies along the Oregon Trail; and to the south, we were passing up Texas, and that's a lot to pass up.

I've never seen the park in the middle of that historic old city of San Antonio and someday I want to take in Big Bend National Park, then drop down to Brownsville and drive along the coast toward Louisiana.

Someday, too: the Ozark Mountains and much of Arkansas—and in Minnesota, Wisconsin, and Michigan: the northern lumbering country that in its day was like a gold boom; then when the lumbering boom was gone, left towns stranded in time. The Middle West has its mining towns as well. They'd all be to the north of where we were going to pass, and at the ends of branches in the road we wouldn't be taking. Another time, perhaps.

Roads lead everywhere through the American past. In any state, and in almost any town, a weekend or a Sunday afternoon drive will turn up any number of timeless places of the unfound, found, or reconstructed variety.

Although it was afoot, albeit lighthearted, that Walt Whitman took to the open road, in his *Leaves of Grass* he sounds like one of today's growing band of shun-pikers: "You road I enter upon and look around! I believe you/are not all that is here;/I believe that much unseen is also here./ . . . From all that has been near you, I believe you have imparted/to yourselves, and now would impart the/same secretly to me;/From the living and the dead I think you have peopled/your impassive surfaces, and the spirits thereof/ would be evident and amicable with me."

# PART ONE

## *The Roads West*

This world, my boy, is a moving world; its Riddough's Hotels are forever being pulled down; it never stands still; and its sands are forever shifting . . . Guide-books, Wellingborough, are the least reliable books in all literature; and nearly all literature, in one sense, is made up of guide-books. Old ones tell us the ways our fathers went, through the thoroughfares and courts of old; but how few of those former places can their posterity trace, amid avenues of modern erections; to how few is the old guide-book now a clew! Every age makes its own guide-books, and the old ones are used for waste paper.

—HERMAN MELVILLE
*Redburn*

1

# WE FIND
# THE BEGINNING

*Down by the sea. A lost road. Navesink, Cross-wicks, Allentown, and Bordentown, New Jersey.*

The night before we started out to follow the "lost" roads, I got lost. Somewhere between the Rumson Bridge and the Navesink River, I took the wrong turn. Mrs. H. said nothing, but I was lost and I knew it, and I was pretty sure she knew it too.

Up at the corner, where the street light struck the leaves of the elms and maples, I tried for a look at the street sign; slowed down, missed; tried again at the next corner; saw the street's name and drove on as puzzled as ever.

It had been about fifteen years since I'd driven these streets, but I couldn't believe I'd forgotten so much. Not that the streets or the houses seemed changed. They weren't. Everything had a familiar look, but I was lost and I felt turned around in space as well as time.

—Like the story about the man who turns down a street he has never noticed before and comes to the door of a garden that stands ajar, enters and finds a mysterious little world, falls in love with a girl, leaves against her sober advice and then spends the rest of his days trying to find that street and door again.

I kept driving, wondering why we hadn't reached the river yet. Finally, Mrs. H. inquired quietly if we were thrashing around in the dark. I told her that like ol' Daniel Boone I wasn't lost, just bewildered. I didn't mention the mysterious turn, the lost street, the lost door. My world of fantasy has become more private year by year; which is what I imagine happens to all of us. When it does get expressed, it's more often than not as comic distortion, as the ironic.

No river, no bridge. Then, with a feeling of disappointment, I saw the road was taking us into Red Bank. As New Jersey towns go, it's a good-sized place; and up to then I'd been enjoying the sensation of being lost in a familiar locale. I think everyone must feel a sense of excitement in finding a section in his home town or home countryside he's never seen before. In New York City where I've come up out of the exit of a subway stop with my sense of direction changed around, the sensation has been bewildering, but never unpleasant. Adjusting the compass in my head, the strangeness went away, a moment of sheer fantasy passed. The same and all too familiar world extended all about me, as I really knew all along it did—and the prospect of a small adventure was nowhere.

On into Red Bank we went, along the neon-lighted downtown streets. I was no longer lost. What was it my father said about neon signs: "If only one couldn't read, how beautiful Times Square would be at night."

Red Bank is one of New Jersey's seventeenth-century

historic villages; but time has moved along the main streets altering the buildings and paving the ground between them. It's grown; accumulated apartment houses, motels, power lines, buses. In short, it's a progressive town. It wasn't, that night, quite what I wanted because I was in the mood of the trip that was to begin at dawn the next day—and that mood was closer to the one that had wanted to find the Navesink Bridge and the country roads on the far side.

Beyond Red Bank, beyond the bridge that crossed the river, we turned left off the highway. Our headlights burrowed the darkness. A strip of road undulated under the beams. The stars were out and under those stars we were the only car on the road. To our right there were old estates that had lawns and slopes that ran down to the river, and on our right there were, between the occasional houses, open fields and trees.

This had been farmland as far back as the Revolution. Much of it, in spite of the growth of cities and suburbs across the land, was still open countryside. When we came to the turn I knew would take us toward the ocean, we found ourselves on a dirt road. It led back across farmland and through woods. Except for the car we sat in, we might have been back in the days of the Revolution—or it could have been later, with Washington Irving, listening to Captain Bonneville spin off tales of Western exploration. It didn't seem as though it could have changed much since then if it was like this now, more than halfway through the twentieth century.

Mrs. H. was leaning forward, staring out at the road. Pebbles and stones caught the white of the beams; shadows shifted, rose up, engulfed. Trotting up the side of the road ahead of us, an all-white dog, short-haired and lean, emerged

35

from the dark. He stopped, looked around, and waited while we went by.

The road slipped down a decline and then rose again. It ran between woods where the columns of the trunks under the solid, floating field of leaves above stood in formation on each side. Under the car a flying stone clicked against us and fell away, fell behind the glare where our headlights spread back the covering night. We were, from overhead, only a moving bundle of light. From behind the eye beams of that light, Mrs. H. said, "One of the lost roads?"

"Sure."

At Navesink, the road ended; beyond Navesink, we came to Atlantic Highlands. At the foot of the pier, beside the boat basin, Mrs. H. let down the table, put the backs of the rear seats across it, and made up the bed for the night. The ocean lapped the dark sands. Before we turned in, I stood where I could see the still lights of a couple of big boats a long way off. They were either heading in or out past the Statue of Liberty, I couldn't tell which.

I got a Coke out of the ice chest and I stood drinking it, breathing the salt air.

I guess I love roads, any kind of roads at all. I've flown in a small plane over countryside just to see where roads begin. I've seen them start as a path in a field and grow to a wagon road and lead to a farmyard and a driveway. They begin like rivers: starting as trickles, growing to creeks—the way country roads join and become the hard, long rivers that are highways. And highways, like rivers, all flow to the sea—where we came from and where, by and large, we'll all return in a good rain some time hence.

There are lost roads. Once I came upon one in a woods, its

old concrete surface adrift with leaves. Weeds and even young saplings were growing from its cracks. And I wondered then, where did such a road go? Where did it go now? I thought of it going off into the past; that if I followed one of those old lost or abandoned roads, I could go back into an earlier time, not only in the life of the land, but in my own as well. I suppose there are lost roads that lead us all the way back to the beginning.

Over in the east, the sun cleared a nebulous horizon. June 22 was a shadowless summer morning. Since a grim predawn hour, even grimmer fishermen had been pulling their cars in beside us; so, along with the sun, we arose.

I started the car and we pulled on down the road where the bluffs began. I got the camp stove pumped and lighted. Inside the car, Mrs. H. was rolling up the sleeping bags and putting them away under the back seats. We had a Volkswagen Kombi Camper. It was to solve any problems we'd have of where we'd stay for the night. It was also insurance at mealtime that we'd have a place to eat since the rear of the Camper had, in addition to a couple of Pullman seats and a table between that turned into a bed at night, cabinets with shelf space.

About the time Mrs. H. was ready, I had breakfast under way. We ate and washed things up; then we took a stroll.

Across the road, beyond the edge of the vacant beach, old dock pilings rose from the water and trailed off across the shallows. It wasn't much of a seaside compared to Maine's rocky littoral, or even to Jones Beach to the north. Along the shore, there was a debris of seaweed, old boards and logs, beer cans and dead crabs.

37

We stood where the water lightly lapped the sand. Looking over the seascape and into the mist, I tried to imagine a British fleet on the run, bottled in, out where I was looking, by the French in the days of our Revolution. The French had cornered them and then couldn't get at them; just snap their teeth and shake a fist or two, that was all they could do . . . out there somewhere. It was hard to picture. I felt a little restless. Beginnings are important but they're hard to make. Endings are easier. Beginnings are best discovered in retrospect; but nevertheless, I hunted around until I found what I wanted. I found an empty bottle of orange soda pop; and I took off my shoes and waded out from shore, and I filled it with some of the ocean before I waded back in again.

We looked around for an old cork but couldn't find anything. There was one we remembered in the car. We walked back, across the sand and through the high thin grass that grows there at the edge of the sea. I corked the neck of the pop bottle, put it carefully away on a shelf and we were ready to start out.

As I turned the car around, I saw a crane had dropped down and was striding about where I'd filled the bottle, taking long, slow steps, lifting his rodlike legs high and setting them down again, looking along his beak with reptilian eyes. Behind him were the dark pilings, like the spine of a sea serpent; and beyond that the mists of a vacuous space that held the whole of an ocean. For that matter, such a mist could have held the whole of the cosmos itself, could have been the one the oldest of the ancient mariners knew lay at the edge of the earth. It was a mist like the firmament out of which the world rolled. A last glance: and then we moved on down the road and into the town of Atlantic Highlands where the doors of the stores were still closed for the night and their windows were the color of mother of pearl.

Navesink is where I prefer to think the trip started—because of the driveway of the house where I once lived and the country road that runs in front of it; but I can't say there was any particular time or place we began. It seemed to me as if we were beginning by moving down a slope from the present into a valley of the past. The Atlantic Highlands and the express highway just beyond were like a ledge that lay along the coast of the Present. When we reached Navesink, a few minutes later, it was along a secondary road, through a woods, and we were already dropping back in time.

I went back, for instance, and very quickly, some fifteen years. I'd last seen Navesink at the close of the Second World War when I was in the Army Signal Corps and stationed at nearby Fort Monmouth. From what I could tell at first, seeing it again, it hadn't altered by as much as a day. It was only on closer look that I saw, or thought I could see, that the roads leading off the main street had been paved. Otherwise: no change.

Navesink was the same. The leaves of the trees along the street and around the houses make a green hill of the town with the houses looking out, under, and around green hedges. They aren't the most ancient houses in the world; they're mostly frame and neat. It's a peaceful little village, a small ageless place hidden away from the rest of the world. I doubt if it's changed so very much since it dropped the name of Riceville back in 1867.

We parked outside the small general store, which is also the post office for the people around town, and we went in and picked up supplies. It was still early in the day. The

39

store had just opened and we were the only customers. We
helped ourselves and were checked out at the counter by a
woman I thought I remembered. Then we went out and got
in the car, and at the corner I turned right and in a moment
turned left down Brown's Dock Road.

This was one of the small roads, off the main street, that
had been paved. I rode my disappointment; the part of me
that resents the impersonal, implacable tick of the clock rode
the road down to the dip at the bottom and the pond and—
then the driveway. There, at the driveway, I pulled the car
off to one side.

It was a long strip of brown earth that moved up a slope
of a hill and back to a white frame house that was older than
the American Revolution. I could see the porch was now
enclosed. It had been open when I sat on it and looked down
the long driveway and imagined it leading beyond the country
road it joined to all the lost roads of America.

"That's it," I said. And Mrs. H. looked back at the road
and said, "Okay, let's go." The lost roads that ran across the
fields of her childhood were half a continent to the west and
ran across Iowa countryside and she was anxious to be off.

The road forked up ahead. The left fork was still unpaved.
We'd driven over it the previous night, and the same woods
came up on each side again. Behind us were white frame
houses, a duck pond, a rail fence with rambler roses; now the
road was dark with shade. It was a windless gray morning, still
slack and resting under the silence usual to early hours of
the day. A left turn on the Navesink River Road took us
along and above the river; green lawns, trees and estates between the water and our narrow road.

The Oceanic Bridge was the one we'd missed the night

before. We found it now down by the river where it had been all along: a nice bridge, a little on the modern side. It's a long span over to Rumson; over we went. Down below were rowboats. In the boats, quiet, immobile figures sat with fishing poles like figures on a gigantic aerial postcard. We turned left and headed east for the ocean, probing our way through the small residential streets with the help of the Monmouth County map.

We crossed the Rumson Bridge to Sea Bright; and then we drove along the ocean front, through Galilee, Monmouth Beach, Long Branch, Elberon . . . an ocean front of great wooden structures of clapboard and shingle, standing three stories high and out of a Victorian era when there was lots of wood and lumber, and a summer home was built to the dimensions of a small palace with turrets and vast, encircling porches and myriad windows shaded by lavish miles of awnings. It's a city by the sea; and it's just about as eternal.

At Deal we turned west and mapped a course through side streets. Beyond Deal and once more in countryside, the clouds that had been threatening rain since dawn broke. We drove through a downpour.

Imlaystown is about 30 miles in from the coast. About halfway there, the rain let up and the sky began to clear. There was no traffic. There rarely is once away from the big highways. The road that swings into that town is a thin black line on the map, Number 526.

We turned from the newer onto the older highway; drove about a mile and came to a village and a time more remote than Navesink. It had, consequently, more of an air of unreality.

Imlaystown is a village with frame houses, all clean and

even freshly painted, along streets that are decades old. The
trees, elm and oak and pine, are big and they shade roof
and lawn and road with a lavender dusk. Beside and behind
the houses are barns built for horse and carriage. Along a
curving length of street are frame houses with flat and porchless fronts that run, without lawn, out to the road's edge. In
the middle of the town is a pond, not much larger than many a
village park or common; and houses, as well as a grain mill,
stand along its grass-green shore. At the coruscant cap's edge
of flat, smooth backyards, rowboats stand at anchor, and out
on the water are cattails and pads of pond lilies.

Sunlight cut a depth across this picture (with brightened
window ledge and oarlock and leaf and darkly shadowed
flower bed and shingle roof and door) that did not seem to
belong to a picture town. The streets were vacant and quiet—
as the streets are in timeless places. Yet people were living behind curtained windows, however quietly and remotely it
seemed to urban visitors; and we felt them there . . . life
moving along, being lived, as we walked around.

The only one who appeared, before we left, was Walter
Golden, owner of the mill which he still kept open and ran
now and then, he said. He was an old-timer around this part
of the state; said the town hadn't changed much. He was born
in 1869. Yes, Imlaystown, he agreed, was a quiet place; didn't
get much traffic or many visitors.

A few miles farther on was another town just as quiet.
That was Crosswicks. On the maps of 1688 when Lawrence-
ville was known as Maidenhead and Camden was Pine Point,
the Crosswicks of then was still the Crosswicks of now. On
the walled grounds in the middle of town where the old
Quaker Meeting House stands is a tree that had taken root

before the arrival in the colonies of William Penn. The meeting house is that of the Chesterfield Friends. On June 23, 1778, during a battle between American and Hessian troops, three cannon balls slammed into its brick walls. One of the cannon balls is still imbedded there. It was through Crosswicks that the British fled, pursued by Washington's forces, before the Battle of Monmouth and the Sandy Hook evacuation.

The Crosswicks of today is fixed in the past—like the little towns inside the glass globes that whirl with snowflakes when you pick them up, turn them upside down, and set them back again. Much of Bordentown and Allentown is also globed securely in former days.

At Bordentown, just across the New Jersey Turnpike, we saw the first of the rows of red-brick colonial houses that we'd see more and more when we reached Pennsylvania.

In Bordentown, along a street where a horse had recently passed, a blackbird lit on the gate of a white picket fence; the sidewalk below the fence was a brick tapestry, uneven, as though it had once flowed and then hardened, grass sprouting between the bricks. Porchless houses came out to the sidewalk's edge, but they were brick now instead of wood as they'd been in Imlaystown—old brick, aging away and mellowing in color.

In Allentown, I thought to myself: The Revolution must be going on; that distant bang can't be a backfire, must be a musket shot. A British or a Yankee town? In whose hands? It was from those days that so much of Allentown stepped clear of time—out of the days when an advancing line of British fighting men could march with such precision that one cannon ball once knocked the rifles from the hands of every man all the way down the line. It was of the days when the officers of both armies played cricket. British officers sold their commissions to pay for their losses at the gambling tables of Occupied Philadelphia. Hessian soldiers sang Lutheran hymns. They sang them when they marched into battle and they sang them as well when they boozed. Horses were quartered in houses when the barns were full-up or none available. Washington's men were marching in rag-wrapped feet, and any man who could come up with a way to make a substitute for shoes out of rawhide could collect a prize of $10. Along this main street, sidewalk, wall, door, and window are still in colonial keep.

To avoid the large and industrial capital city of Trenton and its outskirts, we swung north out of Allentown and then, at Hightstown, turned to the northwest. Princeton lay ahead of us as it had once lain ahead for General Washington in the days when back roads had been back roads indeed.

It was along a back road of uncleared stumps that Washington had moved his men by night from Trenton. The British had assumed him trapped. Fleeing down a lost road? No. He was attacking, as Princeton discovered. It was on his way to Princeton the following day that the Commander-in-Chief of the American forces stood in his stirrups and, waving his hat and yelling like any cavalry captain, led his army after the British. And then Princeton, as he turned his attention there, fell in something less than a half hour.

The Nassau Inn of Princeton has a colonial atmosphere that's awesome, and it emanates from mellow, polished wood and gleaming glass and carpeting. You step back into the time of the Revolution when you enter its doors.

The Nassau Inn was one of our favorite stops on the trip.

44

## We Find the Beginning

We were more worried as it turned out than we needed to be about the eating accommodations with atmosphere we'd find along the way west. There were a good many other interesting stops we made for breakfast or lunch or dinner, and I'll list them all along the way.

We had an early dinner that evening at a place called the Whistle Stop in Flemington, New Jersey. It lay about 30 miles to the north of Princeton; and the year we were moving through when we hit Flemington was, I'd say, about 1910. In this town that seemed to be waiting for a trainload of tourists out of that year stood a curious restaurant. That's what the railroad station had become—as if the town had given up on that trainload of tourists after some fifty years. Old prints hung on the restaurant's walls; the small dining room had menus on a slate; and the prices were "lost" prices. They went way back to a much earlier day.

Out of Flemington, we turned west. Dusk was settling as we crossed the Delaware River at Frenchtown. The first day was ending.

We turned south on Route 32 that ran along the Delaware on the Pennsylvania side, passing fine old brick homes that had been facing the river from the far side of the road since the last stage had rolled by and the barges had moved regularly up and down the canal by the side of the river. We made Stover Park for the night.

Before it was completely dark, there was time for a swim. We went down a long flight of stone steps in our suits and bathrobes and found a few people still swimming in the dammed-up creek. That night in the woods, with no other cars around us, it might have been any century since time began.

45

# 2

# PENNSYLVANIA
# OF THE REVOLUTION

*We dine at an old inn. The plain people.*
*Lancaster ho. The old Amish farmer at the mill.*

On our second morning, we drove south from Stover Park
along Route 32, following the Delaware River along the old
canal. Near Lumberville, we came to a 1745 inn known as
the Black Bass Hotel. Its rooms were loaded with early Amer-
icana and atmosphere, and dining was on a screened porch
with a view of the river.

Beyond Lumberville, just before we came to New Hope, we
turned west; reaching Doylestown, we found red-brick houses
with white window trim and porches and porch railings.
Along the streets there were trees with big trunks and mighty
limbs. It was a prosperous-looking place, on high ground over-
looking farmland. The first settlers had arrived in 1735—and
what had once been narrow country lanes outside the early
village were now narrow streets inside the town.

Just beyond New Britain, we came to one of the remaining
covered bridges in the country. Pennsylvania leads the

other states in the number still in use. It rumbled as we drove in under its roof and came out the other side. Beyond the bridge, we put away the map and struck off on small side roads. We pulled into settlements and small towns without knowing where we were—and once we asked "What town?" of a man walking along the street.

Mrs. H. said, "Are you sure we're heading west?"

In the part of Pennsylvania where we were driving, it was hard to stay for long in anything resembling countryside. Roads covered the land like vines, and houses were springing up everywhere. I pulled over to the side of the road.

Mrs. H. took the compass and got out. She walked away from the car. The sun was bright and hot. We had all the windows open. We were in semi-countryside, and there was a crossroad just ahead. The roads were paved and grass grew high in the ditches on each side. Mrs. H. walked toward the orchard's trees.

The sun was overhead then, and it was hard to tell from the sun where west would be. She balanced the compass in the palm of one hand and frowned. She shook it and read it again.

When she came back to the car, she looked confused and, with mistrust for all mechanical things, said, "Well . . . it says west is straight ahead." She looked doubtful. But we drove on, and the compass kept faith.

There were names like KULP and DURSTEIN printed on the mailboxes we were passing; and in addition to the red-brick houses, the stone homes of the Pennsylvania Dutch were with us now: the first of that careful, meticulous stonework that marks the German settlement all across the land.

Along came Harleysville with its red-brick houses and its porches of white; then Schwenksville with its two-story

47

porches and Georgian Colonial came and passed. Then came two cities, Royersford and Spring City, one on each side of the Schuylkill River. Down the side of one we went (more of the red brick dressed with white) and up the side of the other. Here were a couple of attractive towns, so hidden from the general traffic that I doubt if they're often visited.

Then, late that afternoon, moving west toward Warwick on Route 23, we ran into trouble—a detour. We swung south, down through Pughtown, and picked the first road west we could find. It was unmarked, a country road, pastoral and pleasant, and it led us back into 23. We never did find Warwick. Route 23 was under construction and the workers had gone home. I couldn't figure where we were, but it looked as if Warwick might be back to our right a little way, and I thought I'd try the road, as torn apart as it was. We moved back east, slowly, mile by mile. It was going to be dark soon. We were both hungry and didn't have the makings of a dinner with us.

"There's something," Mrs. H. said.

It was an ancient house and large, over to the left. An inn too—way out in a torn-up nowhere, and it looked open. A dirt road came down beside it to join 23. We turned and took it up beside the house where I stopped, got out and went up and knocked on the back door.

The man who came to the door studied me. I was wishing I'd combed my hair when he said quietly that they were open, but did I have a shirt, tie, and suitcoat.

I went back, got in the car, and drove up the road where we could change. "I think," I said, "it's expensive."

We cleaned up and pulled the window curtains and then we dressed and drove back. By that time, dusk was moving toward

48

night. Inside, candles were burning on all the tables; and for the earliness of the evening and the state of the road out front, the place seemed to be doing a good business. We could hear a bunch making merry at the bar in the next room. The atmosphere was colonial—and intimate: old polished wood and a fireplace. It was expensive all right.

We dined simply, without wine, and walked away for just under nine dollars. But the Coventry Forge Inn was a pleasant surprise, as the Black Bass Hotel had been—and before that the Whistle Stop and the Nassau Inn.

We drove on in the darkness. We moved north to Pottstown and then west. When we got to French Creek State Park, we pulled the Camper over beside the road on a lookout point and turned in for the night.

A wide green countryside lay below us at dawn. We had breakfast and were on our way by 7:15—driving out of the park and turning west on 23. At Morgantown, we took a side road to the left and next a route numbered 122 that dropped us into a valley of farmland and white buildings. Up ahead, a mountain ridge lay across our view in a long bank, a few farms against its greenery. At a curve in the road, a billboard sailed up with words that shouted: *BEWARE LEST YOU FORGET THE LORD.*

When we'd crossed the valley, we started uphill through second-growth woods and dappled sunlight. Then, as the road turned, curving back again toward the valley, we saw coming toward us a horse and a small, hooded buggy.

On the buggy seat, a bearded man held the reins. He wore a straw hat with a broad, round brim. Suspenders looped over his lavender shirt. A woman in a bonnet sat beside him.

49

We turned out to pass another of the same buggies a little farther along the road. The back of the buggy was rolled up and four children sat looking at us as we went by. And then, not far from the road, where the valley began, we came to an Amish farm. It had all the markings.

There weren't any curtains at the windows; and even though power and telephone lines ran along the edge of the road, none ran toward the house. There were, actually, two houses—the bigger one stucco; green shutters on the upstairs windows, white shutters on the lower floor. The stone place, three stories tall, was, I figured, the Grossdaddy house where the old folks lived. There was a hand pump beside that house and a woman stood at the pump looking out at us from under the deep shade of her bonnet.

The buggy with the children in the back came up and passed us. They were girls, all four, and anywhere from seven to nine years old. Of those we could see, one was dressed in green and two had on purple dresses. Their hair was parted down the middle and combed tightly back around their heads. Their horse clopped by. They rolled on down the road, and, framed by the buggy, their curious faces grew smaller and smaller.

Driving on, we crossed the valley and took Route 23 into Churchtown with its old brick houses and its green shutters against white walls.

When we came to a sign beyond town that pointed to the left toward Narvon, we turned. The road was as narrow as a lane and it led between white fences, past a small stone house, to a covered bridge. The bridge was red, and white fencing flanked the approach. An Amish buggy with a boy and his father, each dressed alike, came out of the covered

# SIGNS OF TIMELESS TOWNS

Things a part of the past are still around us: the iron fence.

NEW HARMONY, INDIANA

The millponds.

IMLAYSTOWN, NEW JERSEY

The brick sidewalks.

ALLENTOWN, NEW JERSEY

The iron deer and big lawn.

BORDENTOWN, NEW JERSEY

The railroad stations.

The alley of carriage barns.

EAST BERLIN, PENNSYLVANIA

The small graveyard and old headstone.

The front porch.

The floral stump.

TAMA, IOWA

MONTOUR, IOWA

The vintage car.

The town pump.

OLPE, KANSAS Copyright © 1960 by The Conde Nast Publications, Inc.

SILVERTON, COLORADO

The grindstone.

The popcorn machine.

Opera house.

The footbridge.

BEDFORD, PENNSYLVANIA

The log walls.

KOOSHAREM, UTAH

The board sidewalk.

GOLDFIELD, NEVADA

The town phone.

PARADOX, COLORADO

The unchanged room.

SAN JUAN BAUTISTA, CALIFORNIA

SAN JUAN BAUTISTA, CALIFORNIA

The picket fence.

bridge and rolled toward us; they stared as curiously at us as we stared at them—as though it weren't they who were back in the past, but it was we who were a piece of some future time they'd chanced upon on their way to market. As a matter of fact, we were beginning to feel like visitors from another world, if not some future time, rolling through the Amishman's land of covered bridges, horses, buggies, stone houses, picket fences, and chin beards. We'd become foreign to our own world and time; and being outnumbered, we were for the moment the oddities.

Beyond the bridge we took a turn to the right and drove down the valley. Up ahead was an Amish farmer in his field beside the road, walking behind a horse-drawn planter. Two children sat on the planter, and behind it a third child followed, his eyes to the ground. Like his father, he wore a straw hat and braces crossed against the back of his blue shirt.

A small stream ran through their farmyard and a white duck strolled its muddy banks. We turned to the left and, meandering along unmarked roads, headed for the ridge. We reached the woods again, moved up over the ridge and, coming down the far side, saw a village appear. The curious thing about it was that all the people were Negroes on the porches and in the yards.

I stopped beside a young man who was walking up the road. He was a Negro too.

"What's the name of this place?"

"Pennsylvania," he said, without an accent of any kind in particular.

"The town?"

He nodded.

"Pennsylvania, Pennsylvania?"

He said it was—we drove on.

Down at the bend at the bottom of the road, we came to a house. I parked, got out and walked over to a woman who was hanging clothes on a line in the yard.

"That town up at the top of the hill . . . what's the name of it?"

"Don't think it has any name," she said.

I told her about the boy walking along the road. "He called it Pennsylvania."

"That's our state. That's what we call it."

"I know that. But he said it was Pennsylvania, Pennsylvania, and he said he'd lived there all his life."

She shrugged. "Don't know," she said. "Better ask somebody else." But there wasn't anybody else around.

So maybe it was Pennsylvania, Pennsylvania. There's more than one all-Negro settlement in the United States that sprang up along the Underground Railroad around the time of the Civil War—like Lawnside, New Jersey. It was a good bet this was a similar town: a little historical atoll in a sea of ancient Amish farmland.

On we went, the road winding mildly. At one farm a man swung a great scythe and at another the farmer, in his bare feet, walked along broadcasting seeds from a pail over the plowed earth. There were red and white barns with sloping roofs that were twice the length of the barn's sides. And coming onto Route 340, the oldest paved road in the United States, we turned for Lancaster.

We drove on through the Amish stronghold of Intercourse where the general store has bins of shelled seed corn and peas and four-gallon wooden churns; and then, passing out of the Amish countryside, the town of Lancaster appeared: red-brick houses to each side of us, green lawns between the houses, and overhead, the limbs of big shade trees. There was a Mennonite woman, in a long gray dress and wearing a lace cap, standing on the ground in front of the porch of one of the houses, sweeping a broom under the porch railing. The streets were hilly and a canopy of leaves stayed above us. We drove along one-way streets, past windows with laid-back shutters and window boxes of flowers. There were black iron railings on the steps, and along the curbs of the streets, red and yellow fire plugs.

It was a colorful town dating back to the seventeenth century, though the streets were mapped out in 1730. It's always been known as a picturesque place.

We hung around Lancaster for a couple of days. I wanted to see things to which I felt a remote connection—if only through an old bonnet. I was looking around, soaking in long-gone vibrations left by my Mennonite ancestors.

I thought then about my Mennonite great-grandmother. I'd never known her. But one day, as a small kid, I remember going through the trunks in the attic of the house in Mancelona, Michigan; and I remember coming across some old dresses and bonnets that had been hers. I remember, years later, my grandmother, at the side of a grave in another Michigan town. My grandmother wept quietly that day, remembering a long ago time of her own.

She was living in Grand Rapids then and she'd asked me to drive her to Caledonia. It was the next day when we stood at the graveside and she said, "Well, here I am, Catherine. I've come as I promised." It had taken her nearly thirty years to keep the promise, and I thought at first the tears were as much for the days forever gone as for anything else. But she'd always

53

said how much she thought of her mother-in-law. "I couldn't," she said, "have loved her any more if she'd been my own mother . . ." And all the while they'd lived in the same house, the old woman in her Mennonite bonnets had never spoken a word of anything but German, and my grandmother never anything but English.

I used to think it was funny, that it was the only way to live with any in-laws; but I don't any more. There was, I think now, a genuine bond between them, and buried in the earth at Caledonia was a genuinely loved and good woman.

One morning we drove out of Lancaster looking for a farm that sold home-made ice cream. We had trouble finding our way and it started to rain. It was an odd rain. As the downpour swept back and forth over the fields, we kept driving in and out of it. Sometimes one side of the road was wet, while the other stood dry. It seemed to come down in a patch about a mile wide. We'd see the rain up ahead and across the road, like a semi-solid, and drive into it and drive through it for a while and then drive out the other side into dry air again. I began to think the Lord, so constantly and forcefully present in the lives of the people of the countryside, was picking and choosing who would and who wouldn't get rain.

The farm we wanted was at the end of a long driveway that was more like a road across a field. As we swung into the farm-yard and parked, a station wagon pulled in beside us. I couldn't see any store. There was the farmhouse and beside it a number of farm buildings, and I wondered if you just went up and knocked on the kitchen door.

The woman in the station wagon got out and crossed over to the door of a shed—which she opened and entered. There were no signs around. But it was the shop.

54

A farm woman on a farm had gone into business; that was all. There in the plainest, simplest sort of small store, ice cream was sold by the packed box or by the cone. The Amish lady proprietor, wearing a long blue dress and a gray cap, had a a broad, round face. As I was leaving with the cones, she said, "I make bread, too." I bought a loaf for a quarter.

The next day, driving about here and there, we stopped beside the Ressler Mill which, built in 1760, had ground grain throughout the Revolution. The mill owner was in a talking mood. We stood near the crossroads by the mill and he said he liked to have visitors. He was a thin man with a long, sharp nose and sandy hair. He wore gold-framed glasses, like the glasses I'd seen a Mennonite wearing and I asked him if he were a Mennonite. He shook his head.

He'd been on his way into the mill and said, "Come along." I went up the wooden plank steps behind him and followed inside. Near the door and against a wall were paper sacks loaded with flour and stacked, waiting to be carted off. We walked across the wide boards of the floor that gleamed. It was a big, dusky, orderly place. He was showing me about, lifting samples of pure white stone-ground flour in his long hands when an Amish farmer appeared.

The farmer was an old man and his beard was gray. Like so many of the other Amish men and women I'd seen, he was small and he looked frail; he looked made-up, I thought, like an actor. But as he stood around and I got accustomed to him, I got a different impression. I thought at first I sensed a diffidence and shyness—or was it that here was a man who all his life had worn clothing that set him apart from the rest of the world, and though living among his own kind, he still knew he was different, and remembered that his kind had once been different enough to be persecuted for it?

I thought at first there was something of the hangdog look about these old-timers that others might call simplicity or humility. But maybe it is simplicity—the virtue of the simplicity they practice extending throughout their manner. I watched him talk to the mill owner and he wasn't forward, but he wasn't retiring either. He was, I saw, definitely plausible—a solidly and dimensionally real figure in a thoroughly real setting—with just the amount of make-believe to him that you'd expect in a figure out of the past that had suddenly materialized beside you to no one's surprise but your own.

I'd followed the two of them up the stairs to the second floor. It was a hot day, but the farmer didn't show it. He wore shoes without laces that looked like carpet slippers. His pants were made of a dark, heavy cloth and they were high-waisted and supported by the usual black suspenders over the shoulders of a purple shirt.

The mill owner started downstairs. I followed, and he said, back at the farmer, "Now don't go trying to bring that sack of grain downstairs by yourself." But the old man, I saw, was already getting set to do just that. It must have weighed as much as he did. He pulled it to the top of the steps and then pulled it down behind him, step by step; when it was down to the bottom, he slid it along the floor again and he wasn't breathing hard when he finished. The miller went to work, mixing that and another bag of grain on the floor with a shovel. When he had them mixed, the old farmer held the neck of an empty sack open and the miller started to shovel the mixture in. I saw now how the floor got shiny. When the miller finished shoveling, every last stray bit of grain was swept up with a broom and added to the sack. Then the miller took the pointed end of a file and knelt down and pried grain out of a knothole as well as the cracks in the floor and added that to the sack too. The old farmer watched intently, saying not a word. In his intensity, he was like a young farmer I'd seen in a store in Intercourse adding his bill over and over. Then it was done.

The old farmer turned to me. "There any horses left in New York?" He'd been telling the miller that his horse outside was nineteen years old, and he'd seen, on his way into the mill, the plates on my car.

"A few," I said. "Not many."

He looked surprised and he laughed. "I didn't know," he said, "they had any ragpickers left."

I said I'd seen a horse in the city pulling a vegetable cart not too long ago, and he said he was glad to hear there was still a horse or so around.

The miller hefted the sack of grain over to the door and outside; down by the wagon, he stood arguing with the old farmer. The farmer's wife sat up in the front of the buggy, where she'd sat all the time, looking out under her bonnet. The miller put the sack in the back of the buggy and came back up the steps. The farmer drove off.

The miller said, panting, "I don't like to load up front by the break. There's a sharp rod on the break that punches through the sacks." We watched the high, small gray wagon go down the road, the sunlight glinting slightly on the metal wheel rims and the red reflector.

"For a nineteen-year-old horse, he moves at a good clip,"

the miller said. "Nineteen . . . that would make me in my nineties." He shook his head, as if, even though living among these people, he was still . . . and was it forever? . . . amazed by them.

# 3

WE TURN WEST

*By way of York to Gettysburg. A lost part of the sea. Timeless town after timeless town.*

From Lancaster, we took off for Gettysburg along roads that led us north through a couple of towns at which we took a second look. The first was East Petersburg, which struck me in passing as one of the most attractive and complete "other century" small towns we'd seen. It had backyard barns and back- and sideyard gardens, and the red brick of the homes had faded with age. The houses were a pinkish brick, intermixed with white frame and the town didn't look more than a couple of blocks in depth back from the road.

Manheim followed—a fairly level city set in a hollow of hills, the streets laid out in a regular pattern. The houses on the streets, like East Petersburg's, were white frame mixed with the by now familiar red brick with white porch and window trim. It was a town with a big market-place square, with old stores around each side. Along the streets, there were maple and willow trees and in the yards of the houses there were tall hollyhocks. We saw some women scrubbing the houses. The first was hosing down the side of her place. Then walking along a little farther, we came across two girls in Mennonite dress, lace caps and long gray skirts, and they were out with pail and scrub brush.

We left Manheim by the Mount Joy Road and passed a sign that said the Bible was our road map to heaven. A rim of mountains appeared against the sky; and then—Marietta. It isn't the best example in the state of Pennsylvania Dutch town, but it has some rare old houses and a small attractive square, marred only by a line of parking meters rising from the curb like silver arms with golden mitts waiting for the grab.

We took the road along the river to the bridge that spans the Susquehanna River from Columbia to Wrightsville; and then shortly after Wrightsville, we began to hit some of Pennsylvania's mountain land that was to be with us all the way to West Virginia and the banks of the Ohio River.

Twenty-five miles to the west of the Susquehanna, we came into York, once an outpost of the state and the first settlement to be founded on the Susquehanna's western wilderness expanse. During the days of the Thirteen Colonies, this was the country's "breadbasket," this basin of the Codorus Creek as it crossed York Valley. It's still a rich agriculture area. For a period of about nine months during the Revolution, York was the capital of the American colonies. Between the Revolution and the Civil War, highways bolstered York's economy. The soldiers of the Civil War made a good use of York and York's roads, too. Confederate General Jubal Early swung through town in late June 1863. He was on his way to Gettysburg and he made a two-day halt while he waited for the townspeople to fork over a hundred thousand dollars in cash, as well as supplies for his men. He settled for less and moved on. The town wasn't burned.

Driving through it, we saw blocks of slanted slate roofs and two-story red-brick houses with dormer windows. We saw blocks of old houses side by side and under a single roof; and dormer windows bulging out for entire blocks. There's a statue in that town that's something to see: a Union soldier in full color. He's painted mostly blue with a yellow strap across his cap; he's mustached and carrying a rifle: a foresign of Gettysburg thirty miles to the west.

But we got no farther that day than East Berlin, a town along Route 234 that stands between York and Gettysburg and somewhere between the Revolution and the War between the States. The main street is about a mile long, and there's not much depth to the town beyond the main street.

We had dinner in a farmer's field outside town. When we returned to East Berlin, we parked and got out and walked along the main street. It was the night of the Patterson-Johannson fight and we passed a bunch of kids sitting on the steps of an old brick house that looked at least a couple of hundred years old. The voice of the announcer, excited, talking fast and loud, fading, followed us up the street.

We went into the local tavern and I had a beer. The TV set was on up near the ceiling in one corner of the room, but we couldn't hear the program because behind us, the juke box sang a sad, roaring ballad of the hills.

In the night, with the townspeople out and about, the town seemed to be from no particular time at all. It seemed to be from several separate eras all at once, as though in the midst of the late seventeenth or early eighteenth century, the radio, the TV, and the juke box had appeared—as we, a few days ago,

61

had seemed just as amazingly to have materialized in the Amish countryside. The tavern where I had the beer was early twentieth century, at the corner of a street of homes and buildings out of the days of the Revolution. This was the way it had been, so far, on the trip too: the time of the century shifting and changing outside the window of our car.

The next morning we came into Gettysburg from the north, on Route 34. It was still old Jubal Early's route. He came into Gettysburg with $28,000 of good York money in his pocket; and these were the same fields through which his men had passed. It was substantially the same town ahead. Whitman was thinking of men like these, though on the other side, when he wrote: "We have seen them in trench, or crouching behind breastwork, or tramping in deep mud, or amid pouring rain or thick-falling snow, or under forced marches in hottest summer as on the road to get to Gettysburg—vast suffocating swarms, divisions, corps, with every single man so grimed and black with sweat and dust, his own mother would not have known him—his clothes all dirty, stained and torn, with sour, accumulated sweat for perfume—many a comrade, perhaps a brother, sun-struck, staggering out, dying, by the roadside, of exhaustion—yet the great bulk bearing steadily on, cheery enough, hollow-bellied from hunger, but sinewy with unconquerable resolution."

Along the roads around town there were monuments and statues and cannon all standing, like stalagmites, in honor of one group of men or another who had fought there.

There were cannons of copper, weathered to a robin's-egg blue, pyramids of cannon balls, roadside directions for a self-guided tour, roadside museums; but the nine-tenths of a mile of open field over which the men of General Pickett moved toward the bright rim of Union fire, making their bid and failing, was still open field—without a house, without a mark of change.

We moved west out of Gettysburg, on Route 30, through haze and heat. The foothills of the Appalachians lay ahead. After 15 miles we swung south on a black hardtop road (233) into a high forest. The trees banked each side of the road to the height of fifty feet. We drove upward and at the top of the road, at a turn, there was a pond so full of lily pads it looked like solid green earth at first. We drove on, climbing, through forest leaf and shadow. It was 15 miles to Waynesboro. Mont Alto, midway now to dusk and Waynesboro, was a small settlement of old houses, mostly frame. It seemed to have been a young town in the days of the Confederate and Union forces: a cast to it of, if not the Middle West, of the time of the settlement of the Middle West. It was, like the Union soldier in York, another foresign—this a foreshadowing of a vast area of place as well as time that lay ahead of us. But the architecture of the eighteenth century was not yet at an end; no more than were the "plain people's" settlements all behind us.

We drove over a crest in the road and, with a church steeple over to our right, we moved down into Waynesboro.

It was dark before we settled ourselves in a park on the outskirts of town. That was the night I saw by the light of my flashlight that the water from the ocean was gone. The cork had worked out of the pop bottle. The bottle was empty.

It was just a whim I'd had, looking out over a gray seascape our first morning—something to provide a beginning and an end to a trip I expected would take a long time—carrying a little of our beginning along with us, the way we're told we go around carrying in our blood the salt of the ancient sea out of which we long ago rose. A lost bit of the sea. A lost beginning. Ah, I thought, you can't take that sort of thing to heart. But I felt depressed. I took the bottle by the neck and tossed it off. It spun end over end through the dark and the trees toward a creek I could still just see, and it fell with a splash.

The park where we'd pulled up and where the bottle must still lie is called Red Run. I remember the water from its pump had the taste of iron. We left the next morning under pleasant, clear skies and drove through Waynesboro's streets of brick and frame houses. The town seemed to be built down the side of a slope, the streets slanting up to the north; bay windows on brick houses.

At the end of town, moving west, was a rise—and then out ahead was a yellow field of wheat and beyond that, green countryside. Blue flowers of weeds were in bloom to the right of the road. There was a two-tone green field where alfalfa had been cut, and we could smell the odor of its cut stems.

The big Pennsylvania barns were still with us as we drove across the countryside. In the town we were leaving behind us, Jubal Early had demanded only bread for his men. The road ahead was level, turning in a most leisurely fashion now left, now right—a copse of trees to the left, and to the right a white barn with a weather vane of a horse on the run.

In the town of Shadygrove, I thought the sidewalks looked recently laid; but we were in and out of it too fast to tell.

We drove on through farmland. Ahead of us and almost obscured by haze was a long line of mountains. We passed through Greencastle where the overhead wires were hidden in the foliage over darkly shaded streets. It was 9:15 in the morning, and people were on their way to church, walking down old sidewalks past houses with big white porches.

We ran into some trouble then: the road we wanted, the one that went to Mercersburg was temporarily closed, so we swung around looking for the road that leads northwest to Williamson where we could pick up another road that would take us to Mercersburg. But we were puzzled: there weren't any signs to help us. There, on the left, is that the road? We slowed down; we almost stopped in the middle of the road. No. It led into a park.

Moving along, we came to a better bet. We weren't sure of it either, but we took it: a small, macadam farm road. It took us past an old stone mill—closed, boarded up. The road wound around and around.

At a house on the very edge of the road, two small boys stood at the rim of a low cement porch—faces front: only their eyes moving as they followed our passing. They were blowing up balloons, one with a red balloon and the other with a yellow.

On down the road, there was a cloth hanging on a stick frame and the hand lettering on the cloth read: FOR SALE FRYERS. We took a rise and crossed a railroad bridge and a town, I don't know what, was just ahead. It was an old town: mostly frame houses. Nobody was moving around. In the yard of a school, it looked as if there had been a social the night before. Benches were still covered with crepe paper and littered with paper cups and plates. Above the tables, there were bare, colored light bulbs strung on wires.

It's a lovely old town, of the old Pennsylvania variety: green hedges, big trees, shaded streets, wood frame houses, some yellow. The lawns were shallow as well as deep, the oldest houses having the least lawn.

Beyond town, following Route 16, we came within a half mile of President James Buchanan's birthplace, but the old cabin is gone, packed off to Chambersburg. We went on up the mountains, between bare rock, tree, and grass. Then down. A truck had stopped beside the road and the people who had been in the truck were shooting off fireworks. The odor of the fireworks lingered on in our car after we'd gone by. Past McConnellsburg we went, and on into the mountains.

We had lunch at Sideling Hill Summit at a Blue Ridge Mountain height of 2195 feet. Taking the temporary route west (915) toward Bedford after lunch, we hit still another detour. We rolled northward up 913 toward Robertsdale.

Robertsdale was a small town with unpainted frame houses and vine-hung porches standing along the highway. Here we swung west once more and through small towns where the sidewalks were of brick and often of weed. When they were cement, they were cracked and grass and weeds grew in the cracks.

At Big Broad Top, the streets were wide, the houses were old and there wasn't much shade. It was like a ghost town. Beside the highway, there was an old stone building of beautiful masonwork, all its windows boarded shut. Across the way stood a three story building of hotel proportions. It was almost closed, the windows of the top two floors blinded with green boards. On the roof was an octagonal superstructure topped with a weather vane and the weather vane wasn't the usual one of a horse or a rooster or a fish. It was a gigantic spur. In Big Broad Top, we had another foreshadowing of vaster regions beyond the Mississippi and the prairies. It seemed, even felt, like a Western town.

A few miles farther, we came to a town where the main street stores were along one side of the road, the sidewalk shaded and sheltered by an overhanging second floor, the

66

upper floor supported by iron poles. That was Saxton, an old-time, old-timer's line of store fronts in a mountain town in a mountain setting.

Beyond Saxton, we turned south, following the temporary routing through a countryside of unpainted barns and houses. Another 21 miles and we picked up Route 30 again and turned west and came to Bedford, a town settled in 1750 and the site of old Fort Bedford which had already played its part in history and lay in ruins by the time of the Revolution. It was Brigadier General John Forbes who built this fort and stood off and admired it in the belief that it was unbreachable. His road lasted longer. He needed an avenue west for his thousand wagons and his 7500 soldiers. It's known as Forbes Road today and was when it served so well for the wagons heading westward, driven by the American pioneers. In time, Bedford became a resort town; but the once-popular mineral springs aren't visited as much any more and it has the appearance of a resort town of an older era. It's mostly a weekend town through the summer months. There are lots of old buildings. The Bedford Motel, at least its main building, has had over two centuries of aging.

The Fort Bedford Inn was probably quite elegant in its time. It's been allowed to age, though there are touches here and there of remodeling. She's like a grand old dame keeping up with times.

Beyond town, heading west, the Old Fork's Inn is now closed . . . and desolately haunted at that. It stands at the fork in the road General Forbes laid down in the wilderness. The other road, the one we took, was Colonel Burd's old path cut out in 1775. It's now Route 96. We followed it down along the ridge of Wills Mountain to the bend of Wills Creek at Hyndman.

Hyndman is a town of the late nineteenth or early twentieth century with big lawns, hollyhocks, backyard gardens, and hedges. A sign tacked to a tree in front of a house advertised WORMS.

We stopped in front of the town's drugstore and went in. It was a high school hangout. The town was about the size of the one I'd gone to high school in, and the kids seemed to be right out of my era. That is: no blue jeans and sneakers or ducktail haircuts. The waitress said she had no lemonade but we could have a lemon blend which she recommended. We said okay. The high school crowd sat over by the counter and the boys wore slacks and school sweaters and the girls wore skirts. They all looked relaxed and friendly.

When we went into the drugstore, an old man had been sitting out front and when we left, he was still there. He was in his nineties, at least, and he was sitting in a chair he'd tilted back against the store front, and he had his face turned up into the sunlight, his eyes closed; his cane leaned against the wall beside him.

All the way up the mountainside was a pleasant drive, rolling along beside a creek with a rocky bed, the water flowing fast and white where it hit the stones, the woods ferny on each side of us . . . and once we passed a red barn with a hex sign that looked lacy. It was the first we'd seen of that kind, but driving on down from Glen Savage, between there and Connellsville, we saw some more.

Glen Savage was a town not on our map. We needed gas. A woman came out of the back door of her house and walked over to the pump that stood between the house and the backyard barn. She was in a housedress and apron and she went to work. I asked her what she could tell me about the town. Though she'd lived there for, she said, thirty-five years, she'd never heard how it came to be settled.

We rocked with the mountains the rest of that afternoon— up and down, up and down.

We reached Connellsville the next day, across mountains that were less formidable. It was once, I think, a handsome town; but little had been built here since the 1930s and the downtown looks like the main street of a prosperous community of the first decade of the twentieth century. The streets were once all brick and still are under the asphalt laid at a later time. Here and there, the red brick under the asphalt slips out into the open and rolls its red inlay down between blocks and blocks of old homes. Some of the sidewalks were red brick and once we saw a sidewalk with bricks of a diamond shape, alternating red and yellow. There were homes of yellow brick as well—and one of orange.

Behind town, like a backdrop, lies a ridge of land. Past the town runs the Youghiogheny River. The Shawnees had a village here before the settlers of 1770 arrived. This was once one of the leading coke-producing areas in the world. George Washington was an admirer of its high-grade product. Timelessness is settling in now, and the men in town sit around talking about how much they need local bus service.

Moving west out of Connellsville, we were in coal-mining country. The road undulated through foothills and we passed coke ovens that were like caves of brick beside the road, and we passed through towns of company houses.

Beyond Uniontown, I wanted to get off the main highway and we turned left off Route 21. We hit a country road paved

69

with brick. For a while, we looked at it skeptically, as if in another one hundred yards or so it would roll us into a hidden factory or the outskirts of a village. But there was no town indicated ahead of us, not on our map, and none turned up. The shadows of the leaves of the trees fell across the brick, and where there were no trees, there were open fields, fences, farmhouses, and barns. The narrow brick road rolled on under us, a sort of Wizard of Oz road, except we were still a long way from Kansas. Just where did it lead?

It was old brick, too; nothing recently laid. Passing the farms on each side, we glanced at them, expecting, I suppose, the farms to be the country estates of folks wealthy enough to buy a private job of bricklaying. They looked like good farms, no more than that . . . nothing, that is, quite as special as the paving under us. And then the brick, lasting longer than I'd expected, was gone. We had the usual country road to follow.

The road took us to New Salem. There, the spire of a Russian Greek Orthodox Church rose above its sun-stung clouds of green trees, and on the slopes behind the church there were graves marked by Greek Orthodox crosses.

Along the narrow roads ahead of us, between New Salem and the Monongahela River, there were mailboxes with names like GLUMSIC and CUBIC lettered on their sides. And the people in the settlements through which we passed were all, or so it seemed, blond—tall, stocky fellows with thin straight hair, a wide upper lip, and a jutting jaw.

There's no doubt about it, the river ferries are leaving us. We passed, dropping south along the river, three that had gone defunct. There was a bridge we could take, but it seemed too bad.

Before we reached the bridge, I pulled the car over to a

tavern at the side of the road. Three men, blond with straight hair, wide upper lips and solid jaws, were sitting side by side on the bench outside the door of the bar. They looked me over as I walked up.

I asked about the ferry at Martin. The man closest to me, on the end of the bench, shook his head. "Naw . . . I think that's closed down." The other two nodded and one of them said, "Last Monday."

The first one spoke up again. "You go on down toward Masontown and you'll hit Route 21. You turn right on 21 and you can cross the river by bridge."

"I'd rather take a ferry," I said and they looked puzzled. I went on, "Isn't there a ferry still running anywhere along the river?"

The first one said, "Naw, you don't want a ferry."

"Is there one?"

He laughed then. "I'm telling you, you don't want a ferry. What do you want a ferry for when you got a bridge?"

But he could see I wanted one and he thought I was trying to save money, and he said, "Those ferries cost more than the bridge. You don't save nothing."

I didn't think it would do any good to explain. I said seriously, "I *have* to have one."

"It's a real safe bridge," he said, glancing over at Mrs. H. in the car.

I shook my head. They were thoroughly perplexed. I gazed off and off. They were all silent and solemn now. We conferred again, quietly. When I got back in the car, I said, "I guess we'll have to take the bridge."

"Why were those men all giving me such funny looks?"

I said, "The ferries don't run any more." And we drove on.

# 4

# GREENE COUNTY,
# PENNSYLVANIA, 1865

*A locked door. Lemonade on a porch.*

I found the building, but the door was locked. Inside the door, pressed against the glass, was a card, and it carried the name of the curator. I wrote it down, walked back up the hill to the main street and then along the street until I found a drugstore with a telephone. He was home. When I finished the call, I went outside and stood on the corner because it was time for Mrs. H. to show up. In a little while, I saw her—or rather I saw the car and a coasting span of glass reflecting the sun.

She pulled up beside me and I got in and said I'd found someone who could tell us about the county. "His name is Faddis—he's a colonel."

"Kentucky or Army?"

"I don't know." I told her about the museum; and I thought again of looking back into the room there. I would remember it as a dusky place beyond green shades where relics of the past, in orderly array, had been given over to the keeping of someone living, though absent. The door being locked, the way back was blocked. Nothing lived in there. It was a place where time had not even a breath left, except for the one within myself as I, in one of those inner sanctums, read of some long laid event and saw it revived again. The door had been locked; the curator gone: as are all the doors back to the past. Nothing to do but shake them, try them again, and walk on.

No, of course not, you can't go home again, I said to myself. The past is under lock and key. All that's left is what you remember, what you've heard about it, what you've read of it, what you imagine. You can't open the door and go back.

But, wait a minute . . .

We drove a couple of blocks and turned north and came to a park with big undulating lawns that lay like a lake in the middle of Waynesburg. We drove all around the park and then we pulled over and parked at the west end where the grass and trees swept off and down between banks of stately old houses. Some were college buildings, but they were mostly residential. They were big and old, and so was the park. It was the biggest small-town park we thought we'd ever seen. We got out and started down a slope of grass between trees that slung down shade, and down the slope through the shade we went. We came to a street on the far side; across the street, the park continued. It rolled out ahead of us. It rose up beside us. We followed a narrow walk. At the far end of the park, we came to a fountain where children were playing, and we sat on a bench to watch.

It was a round bowl of a fountain and the kids were squatting in the water and splashing. The youngest was about ten months old; the oldest was six at the most: all in all, about five kids. The father of the youngest was there. He and his wife were sitting on another bench. He was young, and his shoulders were huge, and his neck was thick, and I thought of how the best football players in the country are supposed to come out of the coal-mining regions of Pennsylvania. Greene County was one of those regions. Greene County was in the southwest corner of the state, and we were in the very center of the county, in the county's only town of any size.

The kids were splashing, squatting until the water came up to their chests and slapping their hands down.

For children, age after age, their games, as we know, are pretty much the same, the older kids handing them down to the younger. The hoop set rolling by the first boy rolls on across time, past century after century of hand thrusts, just as the kids are still splashing in the fountain in Waynesburg after many and many a decade.

The fountain in the park was so old it seemed to me if I wanted to wait until after the kids were gone and the grown-ups too, and we were alone, I could walk over to the fountain and look down into its water and see more than I could looking in through the windows of the historical society where the door under my hand had been sealed. In the water in the fountain, grown calm and still, the clouds in the sky would reflect. There would be another sky, another world below, with someone familiar leaning, looking up to me, all the days since the fountain was built floating between us. I could then, it seemed, see more than I had at the door that was closed.

We decided to have dinner at the Fort Jackson Hotel. We left the park and walked back to the Camper and drove toward the main street. It was a small hotel; built, perhaps, in the twenties. Off the lobby, some open steps, guarded by an iron railing rose to an upper level dining room. I liked the Jazz

# FIGURES FROM A TIMELESS LAND

Not only land and houses stand apart from time — but there are people . . .

TAOS INDIAN PUEBLO, NEW MEXICO

BETWEEN LONG BRANCH AND DEAL, NEW JERSEY

A gardener in front of an old mansion.

LANCASTER COUNTY, PENNSYLVANIA

Among the Plain People, the visitor from another time is outnumbered and becomes an oddity in his own right.

At a mill that once served General George Washington, the owner and operator still turns out stone-ground flour.

LANCASTER COUNTY, PENNSYLVANIA

GREENE COUNTY, PENNSYLVANIA

A storekeeper: in his general store.

GREENE COUNTY, PENNSYLVANIA

A farmer: with a horse-drawn hayrake.

GALLUP, NEW MEXICO

Arizona Navajos on a trip to town.

GALISTEO, NEW MEXICO

A couple of cowpokes on the Ortiz y Pino ranch.

SILVERTON, COLORADO

The barber: and his barber shop has changed little with time, no matter where.

SILVERTON, COLORADO

A Mormon sheepherder: Lerell Robinson from Circleville, Utah.

YOSEMITE, CALIFORNIA

Kids go on making rafts and floating them off down old rivers.

Age atmosphere. What were those dresses like? . . . short, yes, and tight; high domes to the hats; feathers. There were victrolas you wound up and then, playing the Two Black Crows or Sir Harry Lauder, they ran down and down. There were victrolas on the porches in the summer and Model-T Fords and ten-cent movies and radios with a pair of tuning knobs. I could remember that much. I was just old enough for memory to start to take hold of the things and the people around me. And now I stood in a hotel nursing a feeling that I might be staring at something that existed below a surface . . . in a fountain, timelessly.

Anyway, we had our dinner and after dinner, about the time dusk was coming in, we drove on over to the colonel's house, and as dusk turned to dark, we sat on the porch and talked. When it was dark, the colonel's wife turned on the porch light and brought out a pitcher of lemonade.

We sat in our shirtsleeves, the colonel and I, and the colonel looked at my map. It was the map of Greene County published in 1865 that I'd found in the New York Library. The colonel was a veteran of World War II as well as World War I, a tall lean man. He said, looking the map over carefully, "Yes, you'll find it's still pretty much the same. It hasn't changed."

It was a warm evening. The ice in the pitcher melted. The colonel looked out over the porch railing, out over the streets where the lamps all across town had lighted. Not much in town, according to the colonel, had changed either, and that was how he liked it.

"Rices Landing? Well, that's not the port it used to be, not any more."

Twenty years after the Declaration of Independence, he said, the county in the center of which we sat had declared

75

itself official. It was on February 9, 1796. Settlement of a peaceful and of a permanent kind had been under way since the Revolution, the settlers moving north from Virginia as well as ferrying in from the east across the Monongahela. The river formed the twenty-five miles of the county's eastern border.

Before the Revolution, the Indians now and then took it into their hearts to chop up a settler or his wife or their children. This discouraged a lot of the pioneers. Nevertheless, by the time Major General Nathanael Greene and General Anthony Wayne had passed their names over to this corner of the state, the territory along the Ohio River was ready to open its fine banks to settlers as well. Veterans, with land for the taking, were thinking about opportunities in that wilderness. Settlers came. Ports rose up along the Monongahela's banks. Rices Landing was a port in the northeast corner of Greene County.

"That's changed some," the colonel said, ". . . no, not the houses. It's just not much of a port any more." Back around the time my map was printed, and earlier, he went on to say, the farmers had driven their stock to Rices Landing to ship up the river on flatboats. And floating along beside them were other flatboats, some loaded with grain, some with whiskey, some with glass and pottery . . . building flatboats in the winter . . . drifting down to New Orleans in the spring . . . drifting down in flotillas, for that was before there were dams . . . fighting Indians on the way down and bandits on the way back.

Before we left, we went upstairs and saw the trophies of the colonel's two wars; then the colonel and his wife walked from the porch to the Camper with us. He was curious about the car. We opened the door in the back and showed him how the table came down and the bed made up. He'd never seen anything like it, he said; and he took in the curtains on the windows and asked where we were sleeping the night.

We weren't sure yet, I told him. It might be over by the park, or we might go on yet as far as Rices Landing. I could see he liked the thought of the trip we were making across the back roads of the county.

Upstairs and at the front of the house, the light was still on in his study where the walls hung with his guns and souvenirs. He was, I thought, able to live more than most of us in a past and a present at the same time—and without one getting in the way of the other, too. They're there to live in.

The past is all around us and not locked behind a door. In *The Croquet Player,* that short book of H. G. Wells about the small, haunted piece of countryside in England, there's a place where the psychiatrist tells the skeptical narrator that animals, unlike human beings, live entirely in the present. Then he continues: "They are framed in immediate things. So are really unsophisticated people . . . But we men, we have been probing and piercing into the past and future. We have been multiplying memories, histories, traditions; we have filled ourselves with forebodings and plannings and apprehensions. And so our worlds have become overwhelmingly vast for us, terrific, appalling. Things that had seemed forgotten forever have suddenly come back into the very presence of our consciousness." To which the skeptical narrator replies—trying, as he says, to keep the man "moored to current realities"—"You mean we have found out about the cave man?" And he gets his answer: "Found out about him! . . . We live in his presence. He has never died. He is anything but dead."

77

# 5

## WHERE THE
## OLD MAP LED

*A patch of progress. Smoke from a cabin chimney.*

At eight o'clock on the morning of our ninth day west, we were at Rices Landing and we were ready to start across the county following the roads of 1865. We drove down by the banks of the green flow of the river where a ferry used to cross but doesn't any more, and we turned the car around and had breakfast. It was a misty morning and no one was up or about.

Then we started, looking first for the road the colonel had told us about, the one where the horses had raced in the old days; but that road no longer ran to the river's edge. It was blocked off from the river, the blocked-off section overgrown with trees and brush. We turned back toward the houses of the town. They showed their age—or more than that, their neglect. It was more of a ghost town than a town living on in the past. There were wooden frame houses, unpainted, and some of them were covered with a tar paper of imitation bricks.

We wound up out of the town on an old road that took us

to Route 88; turned right; and in about a mile came to the road we wanted. It was still unpaved: the old race track. Fortunes had changed hands here. We made our own good time down its five-furlong length and on through countryside where there was only an occasional farm to be seen. So it didn't look as though too much had changed after all. We drove on, and we passed an old brick farmhouse and a little later, a white schoolhouse, and then we came into Jefferson. Jefferson was on our map.

We came into town on a wide street with white frame houses on each side of us. In the middle of town, we pulled the car over and got out and looked around. Few of the houses had porches, but beside us was one that was part of the sidewalk. The posts supporting its roof were cracked and split with age and the roof sagged. Under the roof, the sidewalk was wooden, the planks repaired in places. Across the road was a brick home that had once been a store because above its door and against the side of the building was a sign that was still faintly legible and we made out: GROCERIES, PROVISIONS, HARDWARE. The front steps were stone. They were askew and crumbling. Somebody had tried to touch up and modernize the house with a few incongruous glass bricks, but even they seemed a little withered. There they were, set into an old brick wall, a restive gesture against timelessness, a small rebellious patch of progress. Beneath a lot of unconscious charm rests, as I've said elsewhere, many a disgruntled spirit. But Jefferson had charm. And just a little way down the street, grass came up through the cracks of an old sidewalk like a garden of weeds, and it filled my heart with gladness and maybe a memory or two of small towns in northern Michigan.

We followed a road out of Jefferson that hooked north and

crossed into Morgan Township and then, turning left, we passed through a settlement that wasn't so old. It was Mather. I checked for it on the old map and didn't find it. Time had made a dent here, too.

Now the road meandered southward, and it was dirt; and somewhere between Ten Mile Creek and Love's Hill Cross-road, we got lost. The countryside was mountainous and we got lost up on the high ridges in a wilderness. We drove around in a circle trying to follow the map. There weren't any houses. Then we came out onto a paved road and turned to the west and came into still another town that also wasn't on the map, Khedive. But there wasn't much to the place, and here we turned off the paving for the small country roads again. A few farms turned up, and some of them were brick and they looked old and mellowed. We passed a farm with a buggy out under a tree on the front lawn. There wasn't any traffic along those roads where occasional patches of flowers grew.

I noted haystacks of a type we hadn't seen before. Supported by upright poles, they had the appearance of African huts or even of wigwams and in clusters they looked like small villages. And then we came to a settlement that had been built in the days when protection from Indian villages was needed. That was Gerard's Fort. During the Revolution, a detachment of Virginia militia had kept a refuge there. Even so, the Reverend John Corbly, a Baptist minister, had lost his wife and three children: Indians killed them on a Sunday in the spring of 1782, and the minister had watched it all and barely escaped himself.

Gerard's Fort was an accurately descriptive name for a settlement; and so we wondered about some of the names of other tiny settlements around the county: Live Easy, Little Chicago, Time, Video, Hero, Windy Gap, Brave, Jollytown, Buzz, Gabbletown, Fairchance, Hunter's Cave, and Workman. Jollytown was a name and a place to think about.

From Gerard's Fort, where there'd been some attractive as well as very old frame houses, we swung east toward the Monongahela River, following the meandering country-green, mountain-wild township roads; but a road we wanted (journeying on through a land of timeless and lost and abandoned and vanished roads and villages) had vanished: the road that once followed along the river between Greensboro and Poland Mines. So we swung south of Route 88 to Poland Mines and then, the river view reeling off and falling away behind us, turned west once more. We'd reached the bottom of the county. West Virginia was sliding along my left elbow.

We weren't far then from Snow Creek, site of another Indian incident bad enough to begin with, but not so terrible in its outcome. An Indian, out sniping with his bow, picked off a Dutch settler. His widow and two strangers, neither of whom could express a word of consolation in Dutch, buried him. The widow grieved, to be sure. The strangers, the Horn brothers, were from one of Penn's colonies and Jacob Horn kept a diary. He kept a record of the delicate situation in which they found themselves. Here they were, two strapping fellows with a young lady on their hands whom, if they moved on, they'd abandon to the wilderness and the Indians—and she was determined to stay. Winter was coming. She couldn't speak English; they couldn't speak German. What to do?

They were goodhearted, earnest fellows. They stuck around and helped her out. "Dutchie," as Jacob Horn called her, grieved for a spell and then gradually became cheerful. A couple of months passed. On January 18, 1742, Jacob seems to have brought up the subject of Dutchie, and what they ought to do about her for the first time. They both felt favorably toward her. They agreed on that. And one of them ought to marry her; but which one did she like? Finally John said, "Jake, I'll tell you what we better do. I think we better pick straws . . ." Only here is how the diary records it: "*I, Jacob Horn, do say: How can we say which one she look upon with pleasure. John say: Jacob, break two twills, one some greater in length than the other, hold both before you out of your sight, and say: John take thy choice, by the longer one you shall say, Dutchie you are made my wife by your Bible law. So be it. John make his choice, but ah? He taketh the lesser one. I, Jacob, say, I have no choice, but John say: it must be so, and you Jacob, shall say, by signs, I am to be your man, and John will be our friend, and so be it.*" And so it was, too.

The boys didn't fight it out behind the shed for her hand, nor did the Indians knock off another of them to make a solution easier. They were gentlemen of a bygone day. They picked straws and Jake got her. It was fair and square, and they shook hands. It seemed to have been all right with Dutchie too. Her new husband was a master cooper. He had a good trade, and he became in time one of the judges in the first Virginia court in that region. They had, I believe, a long life and since I found no record to the contrary, I venture they were blessed with many children and much happiness. To-day, our lives are more complicated.

We rolled along to the west, dipped down into West Virginia when we missed a turn, and curved back up into Mount Morris on the Pennsylvania side—and here we followed a little street that led us to a dead end at the banks of a stream. Mount Morris was another old town on the map of

1865, and the past century still hung over it like a hazy, mellow
light slanting past house and yard and dusky barn; and I
thought of that pop bottle I'd tossed away in the dark near
Waynesboro.

We drove on. We were looking now for an old church in a
papaw grove. It was the oldest, the colonel had said, in the
whole of Greene County—lost in a grove of papaws, used as a
barn now. A few years back, he said, the benches and the
altar were still in the church with hay piled over and around
them.

Once we stopped and I got out and went up to a house and
knocked on the front door. Nobody answered. The porch railings were topped with plants in coffee cans, the cans set one
beside another. I went around to the back where a rug hung
over a line, but I couldn't find anyone who might tell me
where the papaw grove and the church were.

I tried a couple of other houses before I found anyone
home and the woman I spoke to said she'd never heard of the
place.

Then we missed a road we wanted. We'd wanted the road
that ran along Little Shannon Run and we swung instead up
to the northwest along Shannon Run. This was a countryside
not of kills, or even creeks, but of runs; and we went up a valley
between steep ridges. We went past a field where a man was
standing in his wagon, driving a team of horses. We passed
high, narrow, white houses and on the porch of one was a
black rocking chair. The valley was green and ancient. Up
ahead was an old log cabin with a stone chimney and someone
living there, smoke from the chimney on the rise.

Then, to our left: a hay wagon in a field and it was horse-
drawn. An old man stood on top of the wagon and a young

man, bare to the waist, pitched up hay from the piles on the ground. And then on down the road, we passed a hay rake drawn by a horse; and all in all, we saw more horses at work than we did tractors.

And we saw log barns; hand-hewn logs cut out of the forests of long ago. We went north, on up into Whitley Township, looking now for a lake that a sign by the road told us would be ahead, but there wasn't any lake that we could find. It had, like the church and the papaw grove, slipped into the earth of a mountainside.

We swung along roads high over valleys and found at last a schoolhouse that, like the papaw grove's church, was committed now neither to prayer nor sums, but to the harvest of the cut stem. The schoolhouse seats were gone, but the blackboard was still in place.

We turned south, looking for a breach somewhere in the mountain's ridges; but there was nothing else to do but to head back and pick up the road we'd missed along Little Shannon Run. We found it at Brock, down by the West Virginia border; and we were then only halfway across the county. We drove on westward again, over small steel bridges, past rusting oil towers, past good farms, past Hoover's Run, past Rush Run, then Tom's Run. We took the road up along Tom's Run toward the northwest. It was midafternoon.

When we came upon Minter Beall's crossroad store, the beginning of the century returned to balance as lightly as a bird on a wire over an era when a good singletree sold for $1.15 and country stores kept their cheese and bacon boxed under screening alongside Gunpowder Tea canisters and Taffy Tolu Chewing Gum. And like the general stores of that day, Beall's was the local post office.

84

I went back out to the car eating ice cream on a stick and woke up Mrs. H. She ate her ice cream staring gloomily ahead. She was convinced by now that Pennsylvania was endless.

But we spent the night in West Virginia on the banks of the Ohio River. At Wheeling Creek Fork we turned southwest on Wagonroad, passed Crook Run and Coon Run, and at 5:30 left the state we'd been crossing for better than a week.

No sign said we'd left one state for another; but the road and the countryside changed. The road got rougher and the woods on each side got wilder. We took Route 250 off toward Hundred, West Virginia—going for a time along a stream spanned by foot bridges, passing hillbilly shacks and large garden patches.

Reaching Route 7, farms appeared and we drove through small settlements, and in one a man, barefooted and bare to the waist, sat on his front porch playing a guitar. With his chair tilted back and his feet propped up against a porch post, he looked out at the road and strummed away to himself.

# PART TWO

## *The Highway that Moved*

There is something in the contemplating of the mode in which America has been settled, that, in a noble breast, should forever extinguish the prejudices of national dislike.

Settled by the people of all nations, all nations may claim her for their own. You cannot spill a drop of American blood without spilling the blood of the whole world . . . We are not a nation, so much as a world; for unless we may claim the world for our sire, like Malchisedec, we are without father or mother.

. . . We are the heirs of all time, and with all nations we divide our inheritance.

. . . The seed is sown, and the harvest must come; and our children's children, on the world's jubilee morning, shall all go with their sickles to the reaping. Then shall the curse of Babel be revoked, a new Pentecost come, and the language they shall speak shall be the language of Britain. Frenchmen, and Danes, and Scots; and the dwellers on the shores of the Mediterranean, and in the regions round about; Italians, and Indians, and Moors; there shall appear unto them cloven tongues as of fire.

—HERMAN MELVILLE
*Redburn*

# 6

## ALONG
## THE OHIO RIVER

*The face on the tombstone. The swindled French of Gallipolis.*

In the morning, we crossed the Ohio by ferry and turned south-west, holding the river in sight. From the far shore, the reflections of the trees along the bank shone out midway across the opaque water. The river flowed between high ridges and there was mist on the hills ahead.

On the way to Marietta, Ohio, forty-five miles downstream, we came abreast and passed a paddle-wheel river boat churning the water. The days of the fast side-wheelers like the *Buckeye State* that ran between Pittsburgh and Cincinnati are gone, along with the fast packet boats like the *Robert E. Lee* and the *City of St. Louis;* but stern-wheelers still move up and down the Ohio, and long stretches of that river look much as they always have.

In one of the series of books on American rivers, R. E. Banta writes of the Ohio: "There still are eddies, pockets, backwaters and bayous on the river which have remained unchanged for centuries; in which the traveler may be hard put to decide whether, through some mischance of time, he may not have arrived in the day of the river pirates, at a quiet moment in the War of 1812 or, frequently indeed, in the midst of the War between the States . . ."

Though the Ohio begins at Pittsburgh and Pittsburgh, since its early days, has been a port for, as well as a builder of, ocean-going vessels, we headed for Marietta. Unlike Pittsburgh, Marietta has remained in a timeless valley, like the valley of the Ohio itself. Its streets are wide and its trees are big, as its houses are also inclined to be.

Back in the early 1820s a Quaker business man from Massachusetts wrote his brother: "The town of Marietta is situated on a delightful plain, almost encircled with rising ground, and at the east of the junction of the Muskingum with the Ohio. It was, until within a few years, one of the most flourishing towns in the state, and even rivalled Cincinnati in the taste and elegance of its buildings . . ."

Marietta has a river museum I wanted to see because I'd heard the museum's outer walls covered, in the fashion of a glass bell, one of the houses of the early settlement. It was General Rufus Putnam's place. He was the man who'd brought the first settlers to shore at this point in the river in 1788.

We parked on one of the wide streets and took a shaded walk over to the museum. The heat was just short of sweltering. Inside the museum, I hung to the water cooler for a while; and then, revived, poked around.

Mrs. H. had gone off on her own. I was looking at a model of the flat-bottom boat the Ohio Company's first forty-eight pioneers had arrived in at Marietta when Mrs. H. came up

and said, "Did you know they almost named Michigan 'Cher-
ronesus' and 'Metropotonia'?"

"They almost did what?"

"It was Jefferson's idea," she said.

I found this disturbing.

We met a little later at a glass case and stared in at a cape
made from the down of milkweed by a Polly Walker before
her marriage to J. J. Fuller in 1815. There was a Paisley shawl
from India. There were some sand toys. A card explained:
SAND SIFTING SLOWLY FROM TOP TO BOTTOM IN THE BOX
CAUSES FIGURES TO MOVE. In one, a Negro in a red-striped
yellow shirt, red vest, and green trousers played a cello and in
the other, a father spanked his little girl.

Inside another glass enclosure we looked at the open diary
of Hope Turner and saw that from Friday, August 19, to
Wednesday, August 24, 1892, Hope had made paper dolls.
She made them every day with the exception of Sunday. On
Sunday she played with them. Little else of her time was
recorded.

In another room there were bearded pictures of the re-
nowned men of the American Revolution—looking like
Amishmen. Then, on an outer porch of the museum, we found
an old headstone bearing this legend: *Here lyes the body of
Able Sherman who fell by the hand of the Savage on the 15th
of August 1794, and in the 50th year of his age.*

Above the epitaph is a face, cut like the words, into the
stone—the face oval as an egg, the eyes bagged and closed.
He was one of the earlier settlers along the Ohio. Southeastern
Ohio was the first part of the New West to be settled because
it was the first land gained from the Indians by title. Sherman

had died just nine years after the treaty that had acquired the land.

On the day of Sherman's death, one of his cows turned up missing and he set out to find her. Indians were still dangerous then, and he took his gun along. It was even likely an Indian had driven off the cow. He searched about the countryside without luck until he finally came to the Waterford Garrison. Nobody there had seen the critter. He said he guessed he'd be starting home, and he was warned he'd better not. Dusk was about to arrive and his settlement was four miles away. But he was known as a stubborn man, and he was characteristically stubborn then. About a quarter of a mile from home, he stopped to gather some apples.

His son in the settlement heard two shots that occurred almost simultaneously. He'd been worried about his father and, hearing the shots, he and some other men grabbed their guns and ran to help. They headed along the trail toward the garrison and there, at the apple trees, lay Able Sherman, apples bulging his shirt; and red as any apple was the stain just over his heart. Where the Indian had stood, there was a trail of blood for a little way on the ground and then it was lost.

The white men the Indians hated most were the ones who came and cleared a piece of land, put up a house and then *built a road*. They didn't mind the white men who hunted and fished and traveled their land nearly so much as those road builders. They could even put up with a small settlement or two—provided the people gathered in the settlements didn't build roads. For in such roads the Indian saw not merely danger but disaster.

The early explorers and exploiters of the wilderness had moved mostly by water. The Ohio was the Big Road West.

Then roads began to appear across former Indian land. First, the red men had had the wilderness and the game and Indian trails to themselves. Then through the wilderness appeared the white man's tote roads, pack roads, and avenues for wagons.

The road builders were to doom the river boats, like the *J. M. White*, in time too. There were models of a number of river boats downstairs in the Marietta museum, the *J. M. White* among them. She was an elaborate piece of grandeur from the years before the Civil War: a big white boat with gold trim and tall, black twin smokestacks with tops that were like crowns.

One of these old river boats, now a museum piece, was pulled up at the edge of shore in Marietta and for an admission price could be boarded and examined. We had it all to ourselves, the *W. P. Snyder, Jr.*, so I could imagine the *J. M. White's* pilot room. There would be a pot-bellied stove with a shield that could be moved around to direct the heat where it was wanted. A big megaphone was handy for the pilot or the captain, and up over the top of the stairs was a bench that I guessed was for visiting pilots.

Anyway, it was man-made roads of one kind or another that brought the Ohio's traffic (the big five-deck river boats with chandeliers of cut glass, miles of gleaming brass and wood, sofas of velvet and goosedown, and vermilion and yellow and lavender carpets) into a decline—the canals and the railroads and, finally, the white man's highways, like Zane's Trace and the National Road.

By the time the Western movement of the population reached the banks of the Mississippi, the railroads in the East and the Middle West were replacing the canals. That was at the beginning of the second half of the nineteenth century.

93

The canals, so recently completed, were already outdated and the stagecoaches were getting fewer and fewer. But even so, doomed or not, boat traffic was still moving huskily up and down the Ohio. All along the Ohio, the river towns were booming. Among other things, the Ohio Valley was a cattle-man's country. Corn and wheat were raised and shipped. Lots of hogs were raised and butchered too, and many of the towns along the river were meat-packing centers.

The first steamboat, the *New Orleans,* had appeared on the Ohio in 1811 and the next year a river commerce began on which the West would depend until the time of the Civil War. After the war, it was the collapse of the river trade, the star of the iron horse on the ascendance that clamped ridges of timelessness along each side of so many of the Ohio River towns. Progress—change—went on to the north of the river; and as the industrial towns of Detroit, Toledo, and Cleveland grew, many of the river towns seemed to be waiting for the great throngs of river men and boats to churn on back again.

There are a couple of places we found to eat and stop over in Marietta. For one, the Hotel Lafayette: conventional-look-ing from the outside; wall-draped and pine-paneled inside, with a dining room decorated with flintlock guns. The Betsey Mills Club, for another, seems closer to New England than to the riverboat days, but has charm nevertheless. Rooms are only for women, but the dining room, with its good in-expensive food, is open to the public.

We didn't stay around town for the night, however. For the first time since we started the trip, we drove on after dinner, in darkness. I figured there were going to be factories just ahead, and I felt they'd fracture more than they'd help the mood of the trip. And so we had a passing view of a nearly lost and gone splendor on the river: a packet boat, its lights all on, floating down the dark river like a constellation of stars, like the big dipper itself coasting along upside down.

All up and down the Ohio River, the past still exists, as it does in the museum in Marietta—one decade, that is, comfortably beside another, and including in its tickless, timeless span of years the French busily burying lead plates between halves of stones. That was in 1749 when they were claiming the land for their king. And the French, still interested, settled Gallipolis about one hundred miles downstream from Marietta in 1790.

We headed there next, keeping the river to our left where it flowed along greenly, gracefully between banks regrown with trees. Route 124 was small enough so there was no white center line. Near Hocking River, we passed a post office in a log house with a faded flag, and we rolled on down a valley of foliar arms, between arms in the green sleeves of trees; past escarpments the color of sawdust; rolling along . . . Racine . . . Pomeroy . . . Middleport . . . Gallipolis.

Thirty years after a bewildered, thoroughly swindled group of French Royalists settled Gallipolis, an Englishman by the name of John Woods passed that way and after describing the town as "pleasantly situated on a high bank," went on to note: "On a green of good land, near the town, a motley flock of sheep was feeding; many of them had a rotten appearance. I was told they belonged to the inhabitants, who kept them in common. The green on which they were was good sound land, but as they had free access to the river banks, they often fed on herbage that was frequently under water."

That was thirty years after, and those sheep must have been like a macabre codicil to the legacy of the original five hundred settlers, something malevolent left lingering on. The poor devils had found on arrival that they didn't own any property along the river because they'd bought it from a company that didn't own the land they were selling. Five hundred stranded adults and children; but the Ohio Company gave them land to settle on and even built them a fortification. The town began. But they, the settlers, didn't stick around for many years. They weren't farmers to begin with. They moved on, some to Detroit, some to St. Louis. By 1807 only twenty families were still there. Settlers from the eastern seaboard were then moving in and setting up homes. Nevertheless, the town still celebrates the day Lafayette paid them a visit.

Another distinguished visitor from France visited the town before Lafayette. In 1795 the man who later became King of France, Louis Phillipe, slept in a bed now a museum piece in Gallipolis. Napoleon Bonaparte was interested in the French settlement too. It was, as a matter of fact, his plan to found a French Empire in America; but as reports came back to France that the colonists were having a rough time of it, he changed his mind.

There was famine and scalping and suffering. It wasn't the land of lemonade springs and singing bluebirds they'd been promised. The fish didn't jump into their pockets, and game was scarce.

A picture of the town in 1881 shows the river banks where the settlers had their cabins, sloping down to the water as they do today. In the park, however, the cabins are gone. In and around town is many an old brick building—the most we'd seen in any town since we started down the Ohio. A few were painted white.

Running east off the park and along the river is a street of houses that are all early nineteenth century, some frame, some brick. This is First Street, and it's like streets we saw in New Jersey's early American villages.

It was along here on the river that the young George Washington ended his Ohio journey. When he returned East, the proximal river valley of the Kanawa stayed on his mind; and when, during the Revolution, the prospect of victory looked bleak, he proposed, in event of defeat, this Ohio country be the new seat of the American government. First Street is a fanciful strip of what-might-have-been had it not been for the help of France, superimposed along the river in a town settled by the French a little after the Revolution.

At Portsmouth, in a tangle of industrial towers, tracks, and trucks, we crossed the river into the "dark and bloody land" of Kentucky. We'd been on the road then for eleven days and we'd covered no better than 1500 miles.

# 7

# ALONG BOTH BANKS
# TO NEW HARMONY, INDIANA

*Maysville. Vevay. Madison. Unmarked graves.*

Moving along Route 10: industry disappeared; we dropped back into the past once again. There was less traffic and there were fewer road signs. Cattails grew in the ditches beside the road and over on our left were the flanks of steep, conical hills. To our right and below, the river flowed between banks with trees that grew as high as thirty feet or more.

The road took us on into Vanceburg, Kentucky, across some railroad tracks, and in among houses out of my grand-parents' lives; the few people we saw on front porches or in the yards seemed to be grandparents too. Between the houses, corn stretched from clapboard wall to clapboard wall and grew in rows to the edge of the street. Up ahead, an old man came out of the back door of his house and, carrying a pail, came down a a short flight of steps and walked toward a hand pump.

On our way to Vanceburg, we'd passed through several similar, though smaller, settlements with white houses, gen-

# FROM THE ATLANTIC TO THE OHIO

"... carrying a little of our beginning along with us, salt of the ancient sea out of which we long ago rose."

ATLANTIC HIGHLANDS, NEW JERSEY

SEA BRIGHT, NEW JERSEY

"... an ocean front of great wooden structures of clapboard and shingle..."

". . . a tree that had taken root before the arrival in the Colonies of William Penn."

QUAKER MEETING HOUSE, CROSSWICKS, NEW JERSEY

NEW BRITAIN, PENNSYLVANIA
"We came to one of the remaining covered bridges in the country."

Heading West.

NEW BRITAIN, PENNSYLVANIA

"There weren't any curtains at the windows ... The stone place was,
I figured, the Grossdaddy house where the old folks lived."

AN AMISH FARM; LANCASTER COUNTY, PENNSYLVANIA

The word of God is "constantly and forcefully present in the lives of the people of the countryside."

". . . I remember coming across some old dresses and bonnets."

LANCASTER COUNTY, PENNSYLVANIA
A barefooted Amish farmer at work in his field.

EAST BERLIN, PENNSYLVANIA

"Three houses made left to right stations to the past: Civil War, Pennsylvania Dutch stone, Colonial."

The Pennsylvania Dutch had and still have their own ideas of the way a barn should look.

"... the great bulk bearing steadily on, cheery enough, hollow-bellied from hunger, but sinewy with unconquerable resolution."
—Walt Whitman.

BARLOW'S KNOLL, GETTYSBURG, PENNSYLVANIA

"There were cannons of copper weathered to a robin's egg blue, pyramids of cannon balls ..."

GETTYSBURG, PENNSYLVANIA

A bullet hole in the whitewashed outside wall of General George Meade's two-room cabin headquarters.

GETTYSBURG, PENNSYLVANIA

Battlefield relics.

GETTYSBURG, PENNSYLVANIA

BEDFORD, PENNSYLVANIA

Credited to the early Swedes.

Old Forks Inn on the Forbes Road, built in 1764.

OUTSIDE BEDFORD, PENNSYLVANIA

". . . All in all, we saw more horses at work than we did tractors."

". . . they had the appearance of African huts or even of wigwams and in clusters they looked like small villages."

"There wasn't any traffic along those roads where patches of flowers grew."

GREENE COUNTY, PENNSYLVANIA

GREENE COUNTY, PENNSYLVANIA

"... when a good single-tree sold for $1.15 ..."

# DOWN THE OHIO

MAYSVILLE, KENTUCKY, ON THE OHIO RIVER

"On the way to Marietta, Ohio . . . we came abreast and passed a paddlewheel river boat."

MARIETTA, OHIO

"One of those old river boats, now a museum piece, was pulled up at the edge of shore."

"Where the Indian stood, there was a trail of blood along the ground for a little way, and then it was lost."

"We passed a post office in a log house . . . and we rolled on down a valley of foliar arms . . ."

NEAR HOCKING RIVER, OHIO

Sometimes the rain transfigured a town with the gray shimmer of a yesterday from as far back as first recollections, and gates hung open as though leading to that time.

BUENA VISTA, OHIO

The whole town looked as if it had just been painted white.

MAYSVILLE, KENTUCKY

MAYSVILLE, KENTUCKY

"... the pleasant cool splendor ..."

MADISON, INDIANA

"The stores along the main street are from the last century, and overhead there is no clutter of wires."

"What remains . . . today is, by and large, a Rappite town . . ."

NEW HARMONY, INDIANA

The courthouse at Mt. Vernon, Indiana.

OLD SHAWNEETOWN, ILLINOIS

"Down by the river, flat-bottom boats sold catfish . . ."

# BEYOND THE BANKS OF THE MISSISSIPPI

"We might not remember the pioneer days, but our grandparents did, and we remember their memory of it."

INDIANOLA, IOWA

TAMA, IOWA

"We agreed that no one who had not grown up in a little prairie town could know anything about it. It was a kind of freemasonry, we said."
—Willa Cather.

TAMA, IOWA

"Oak Park is shaded and quiet . . ."

"By the sidewalk . . . a fountain . . ."

TAMA, IOWA

"White frame houses have lateral clapboard lines that show as dark, under the sunlight, as charcoal pencil strokes."

TAMA, IOWA

". . . and closed his fingers into fists and tugged, as if he were pulling in bids from those passive faces above him."

TAMA, IOWA

MONTOUR, IOWA

We went on through small prairie towns.

6:15 P.M.

ALMA, KANSAS

"Folks in farm clothing . . . were walking about . . . an enclosed wooden stairway ran up along the side of an old general store."

OLPE, KANSAS

WOOD, KANSAS

Grain elevators rose like strange towers . . .

NEAR MEADE, KANSAS

. . . and castles. The Land of Oz did not seem far away.

eral stores, and small gasoline stations: old communities with outhouses still standing in backyards.

Next, Maysville, Kentucky, seemed almost entirely white, and as though it had just been painted. The pleasant, cool splendor of this town continues year after year. Not only had Maysville been an important and a prosperous river town, it was a hub for the earliest highways. Three roads met in Maysville—the Wilderness Road that dropped south to the Cumberland Pass; Zane's Trace, just across the river and swinging north and east through Chillicothe, Lancaster, and Zanesville, Ohio, on its way to Wheeling, West Virginia; plus a branch of the Natchez Trace that led through wilderness and forests of pine and sand all the way to New Orleans.

All such early roads, and there were many others, held the promise of present-day cutoffs left by highway improvements; and on those cutoffs, timeless towns. I imagine the old National Road (now U.S. 40) that ran from Cumberland, Maryland, to Wheeling and on across Ohio, Indiana, and Illinois toward St. Louis must have a roadside full of lost villages. And the old Michigan Road that ran north and south in Indiana from Madison to Lake Michigan must make Indiana's present Routes 7 and 31 interesting exploratory driving. For the sake of time, however, and of keeping on course, we had to pass these up.

We drove on west out of Maysville, past the estates on the hillside facing the river: beautiful old places. Men with a liking for Georgian Colonial, for pillars and green shutters built along here. And then we decided to take the bridge, which can be seen from that drive, across the Ohio and downriver to Ripley. We wanted to bypass Cincinnati on the Ohio side.

John Woods, the Englishman previously quoted, passed Ripley on his way down the Ohio and wrote: ". . . A gentleman who had joined us at Maysville, and my eldest son, went onshore near this place. My son purchased two quarts of milk, for which they charged him 25 cents; he promptly demanded his money again, and offered to return the milk; this they refused; he then gave them, as he called it, a good *blowing up*, and came on board in a very bad humor, not being at all pleased with his bargain."

At Ripley, where Eliza with the hounds at her heels was supposed to have crossed the ice in *Uncle Tom's Cabin*, we had dinner in a small park. After dinner we drove north and pulled over for the night at Grant Lake.

When we woke up early the next morning, there were already cane pole fishermen out on the lake in small rowboats; and while we made and had breakfast, a woman in a sweater and an old hat with a brim that came down and shaded ears and eyes watched us with binoculars.

That morning we circled Cincinnati, passing through towns that were settings for Sherwood Anderson's *Winesburg, Ohio*: Greenbush, Fayetteville, Owensville. Fayetteville was a neat, old-fashioned town—without industry. John L. McCaffrey, the president of International Harvester, came from there. His father owned and ran the hardware store across the street from the post office. Bill Jordan is the postmaster and Naomi Brulport his assistant. There are eighty boxes. The fire department is volunteer, has eight pieces, and they have a hand-operated fire pump that still works.

We came back to the Ohio River again at Rising Sun, left town past a garage with a lilac bush that grew above the rooftop and drove out along a curbless street.

At Vevay, Indiana, an old post town and the capital of Switzerland County, I stopped to buy some wine. This town, settled in 1814 by some French-speaking Swiss from Pays de Vaud, was once famous for its vineyards half a mile below town.

Age had done some withering in Vevay, and though the withering, along old streets of houses, was interesting, the wine it was once famous for had evaporated beyond even the taste of the townspeople. In the local liquor store, I tried to get some burgundy.

"No calls for it," the man said. "Just port and muscatel, that's all anyone ever buys."

But we were back among the river towns again, in a dog-eared sort of past. We drove on to Madison figuring to have dinner there and spend the night.

"Madison," I explained to Mrs. H., "will be the kind of town we're looking for."

"Our kind of town?" She's a needler, but nice.

"That's right. That's Madison," I said. When the commercial traffic on the Ohio had been at its peak, Madison had been the biggest and the dandiest city in the state. It was Indiana at its best: the finest homes, the finest shops. And then progress kicked the props out from under it all. The Michigan Road and the National Road, crossing at Indianapolis, did better for Indianapolis than the river could do for Madison. It was as though the river had taken one of the changes in its course that Mark Twain described. Madison was as good as isolated.

There's a street in Madison called Broadway and that's where the old days are. It's an exceptionally broad street, partly boulevard and several blocks long, as it runs from the river back across the main street and into the town. Behind the shaded sidewalks and iron fences, set back across lawns, are old homes with shutters beside the windows. There are doors with fanlights and there's a fountain that lights up at night on the block with the boulevard.

But the old days are elsewhere, and in force as well. The stores on the main street are from the last century, and overhead, there is no clutter of wires.

We found a room for the night in a tourist house across the street from the Lanier Mansion, the home in the "good old days" of the richest man around, in a town, from the look of Broadway, that had a good many well-to-do folks.

We bathed and dressed for dinner. It was evening by the time we were out on the street again. We took a walk along the lawns in front of the Lanier Mansion, and then down the side of the grounds to the river. It was a pleasant evening, and we strolled around for a while and then went back to the car.

So it was about nine o'clock when we drove up to the Hillside Motor Hotel where the dining room has a pleasant view of the river. The dining room was closed. And so were all the other restaurants in town! The towns along the river, we found out then, all close early; and along the streets of Madison that night, as we walked hungrily from block to block, not even a chromium-trimmed hamburger shop shone out to comfort us. And there was nothing to cook in the car.

The next day we recrossed the Ohio. We took a ferry over to Brandenburg, Kentucky. Near the road's end at the river's edge, there were some swimmers we watched while the ferry loaded. Swimmers were something else old John Woods noted on his Ohio trip. He said it was ". . . the first thing that strikes a traveler on the Ohio . . . the immense number of children, many of them almost naked. They do not appear healthy; but they look happy, rolling in the water and dirt. We often saw little boys swimming in the river, sometimes leading others that could not walk: thus the dread of water wears off while they are very young. I never heard of any of these children being drowned."

He also noticed the richness of the Indiana soil and said of it: ". . . so rich that the Indian corn was the largest I have ever seen; the owner said it was eighteen feet high, but I think he made the most of it. I picked up a stick about six feet long, and, by measuring it with that and my own height, I should judge the highest of it was from 14 to 16 feet."

When we pulled out from the shore, the ferry made a complete turn, end for end—and down the river, passing us before we'd crossed, came *The Delta Queen*, stern-wheel river boat. It boomed up the middle of the river, moving upstream, fanning a wake out behind it that reached, faintly, from bank to bank.

Brandenburg was a tough little river town in the old days, and it didn't seem to have changed much in appearance. We drove uphill along a Main Street of stores: old frame buildings with porch roofs supported by iron poles. The residential part of town was on higher ground.

We left town on Route 228 which followed along above the river for a short distance. After a time, we hit a dirt road. Just ahead of us was an old car with cane fishing poles tied to the roof. The fields of Queen Anne's lace on each side were like green waves and spindrift.

At Owensboro, Kentucky, we were getting into the South. Every day since we'd left Marietta, the river had been dropping steadily into areas where the drawl of the people was

becoming more and more marked. Except for the courthouse in Owensboro, I couldn't quite say where the look and
the feel of the South came from, but it was present.

From Owensboro, we followed Route 60 to Henderson,
Kentucky, a town where John J. Audubon lived for nine years;
and the following day crossed the river and took Route 66 for
36 miles to New Harmony, Indiana.

John Woods also visited here and reported on it when it was
known as Harmonie: "Harmonie belongs to a society of Ger-
mans, here called Dutch, under the direction of Mr. Rapp
. . . This society now consists of upwards of eight hundred
members; they carry on many branches of business . . .

"Each lives at his own house; but dines at the same hour,
and I believe all take their meals in the same manner . . . The
Reverend George Rapp is their priest . . . Many of the buildings are of logs; but there are some good brick houses, and a
neat frame church painted white, with a large clock."

There are many old buildings from the early half of the
nineteenth century: some restored, some not. It remains a
small, attractive town, deep in the mood of its past.

We stood the longest looking into the Rappite Burial
Ground where there are no grave markers and the grass is
carefully cut over an expansive piece of earth surrounded by
brick walls.

As long as Rapp lived to lead this group of German Sepa-
ratists, they thrived. They certainly hadn't failed when Robert
Owen came along in 1825 and bought them out. They'd had
many good years of it and then, turning it all over to Owen,
back to Pennsylvania they went to set up still another, their
third, colony in America. Robert Owen, the new landlord, was
a wealthy Welsh industrialist and an idealist, bent on found-

ing an "ideal society" in America. He plunked down $182,000 for Harmonie's buildings, livestock, and 28,000 acres, and then extended an open invitation to all settlers who were ready and willing to follow his high-minded principles of togetherness. Settlers packed in. Within six months, he had a thousand followers on his hands. They were sincere enough. There was just a little too much scattered leadership and enthusiasm. They fought and haggled, to begin with, about the constitution. They formed splinter groups. Within a year, the road that Owen had paved with hard cash and the best of intentions had gone to hell.

What remains in New Harmony today is, by and large, a Rappite town with traces of Owen's residence here and there. Words of Owen in open-air evidence ironically read: *"If we cannot reconcile all opinions, let us endeavor to unite all hearts."* At the age of eighty-two, and considerably poorer, he turned to spiritualism.

# 8

# THE END OF THE
# RIVER AND AN EPOCH

*A tough old river town. The river pirates' cave.*
*Cairo, Illinois.*

From New Harmony, we moved back toward the Ohio River
by way of Mount Vernon, Indiana. Then, crossing the Wabash, we came to Illinois and turned south down a road with
sunken fields of corn on each side.

The wilderness of John Woods' day had run from the East
all the way to the Wabash, and out of the wilderness and
onto the beginning of prairie had come men who, swinging
broadaxes weighing up to ten pounds, could take off the side of
a log as straight and slick as a saw would in years to come.
They were trained in a fine art the wilderness had taught
them, which was soon enough to become unneeded and lost.

Settlers kept moving steadily westward down the Ohio, and
many of those on the river boats got off at Shawneetown,
Illinois, and took off across the southern part of the state for
Kaskaskia, St. Louis, and the Mississippi River.

John Woods disembarked at Shawneetown to make his way

inland to the English settlement at Albion. He had some supplies to buy and he was around town for a few days and had this to say of it: "We purchased a few articles to take with us, as we understood they were difficult to be procured at the Prairies; they consisted of an iron stove, some articles of grocery, etc. Many of the store-keepers were very obliging, but the boatmen the very reverse; a rough set of men, much given to drinking whiskey, fighting and gouging, that is, they fight up and down, trying to put out each other's eyes with their fingers and thumbs, and sometimes biting off each other's noses or ears. A man who resides near me, had the top of his nose bitten off, in one of those brutal frays, some years since. This is their common manner of fighting; but it is said that the neighborhood is improving in buildings and manners."

The next day he recorded: "This was the Sabbath, but not much observed at Shawneetown, there being no place of public worship. The Methodists sometimes hold meetings in a private house, but they are not well attended. There was much drinking and fighting, nor was work wholly laid aside, as we saw several teams out."

Shawneetown, now "Old Shawneetown," is still a wild and lawless-looking place (and not to be confused with the newer and vastly more respectable-looking Shawneetown located back from the river, on the bluffs, along Route 13) with main street saloons set side to side. The streets were unpaved and full of holes. And the houses there, old and big, mansions some of them, had gone to pot; but they were still in use with curtainless upstairs windows at which the shades were drawn. There were houses with brick foundations and slate roofs and big yards surrounded by iron fencing. And in among the paintless, faded frame buildings along the town's unpaved streets, there were some once-dignified brick houses. Down by the river, flat-bottom boats sold catfish and swimmers were out in the river. No one had changed Old Shawneetown, or kept it up for the tourists, and all over town the trees, the streets, the houses were charged with a past that simmered below bark and wood and brick and stone.

Old Shawneetown is located along a stretch of river between Evansville and Cairo that was as lawless in the early nineteenth century flatboat days as any part of America; and families on flatboats, making the 15-day float from Pittsburgh to New Orleans, passed that stretch of river with their guns loaded and cocked.

Strictly speaking, the dangerous run began at Owensboro, then called Yellow Bank, Kentucky. Below it lay Red Bank (now Henderson, Kentucky), Diamond Island, Cave-in-Rock, Shawneetown, and Wabash Island; and they were crawling with outlaws like Colonel Plug, Mason, and the Harpe brothers—figures that struck a chime of terror and sinister beauty in the imaginations of boys like Huck Finn and Tom Sawyer.

The Harpe brothers, besides being highwaymen and murderers, loved a little joke—and as though to prove they were human in this respect, they once tied a victim to the back of a horse and drove the horse off a cliff. The joke was not only on the man tied to the horse; it was also on the men sitting around a fire at the bottom of the cliff. This cliff was the one over the entrance to Cave-in-Rock; and the men below were the outlaws who lived and hid-out there. They not only saw precious little humor to the horse that dropped into their midst, but they hastily black-balled the Harpe boys from their smoky society.

*The End of the River and an Epoch*

The cave, now in a state park area, is about twenty miles downstream and around a bend in the river. Just past the opening, the cave gets larger, the inner walls stratified and brown. It's big enough to accommodate a regiment of bandits; and they could cook in it, too. A fissure in the ceiling seemed large enough to carry off smoke and to provide a shaft of daylight. It's a cool and a dark cave, and no one else was inside ahead of us the day we went for a look; it was as cool as the hand of a dead man.

Driving on to Golconda, about twenty-five miles away, we came to a town founded by a woman in 1803. She ran a ferry service, with the help of a young son, a colored woman, and a rifle. For a long time, the town was known as Sarahville. It's a quiet place today, still back in another century.

The next day we came into Cairo on Washington Avenue, a leaf-darkened, brick boulevard; and drove past the Magnolia Mansion, built, like so many of the big homes in the town, at the end of the 1860s when Cairo was challenging Chicago as Illinois' urban summit. Today, the population of this terminal Ohio River town, which the natives pronounce "Kay-row," is not much more than 12,000.

General Ulysses S. Grant put up briefly as a guest at the Magnolia Mansion before establishing his permanent headquarters at the St. Charles Hotel in Cairo. In those days, recruits for the Western campaign were overflowing the town and onto boats; and Grant, from his hotel room, watched the men drill day after day.

Grant's room and his private bar, in the hotel wing that burned, no longer exist; but the Hotel Cairo has its lobby walls papered with a silver-striped wall covering ordered originally for the St. Charles. The Hotel Cairo has recently been remodeled to look like the nineteenth century and has a few rooms furnished (to the smallest detail) circa 1830—and that includes beds put together with wooden pegs, and on the book shelves, Annie Randall White's old *Etiquette Book*. We had some channel catfish for lunch at the hotel and it was good.

As in all the river towns along the Ohio, there was a curious glitter and glint the eye almost caught, and a sound the ear could almost hear—like, for one thing, the sound of the carriage in which Teddy Roosevelt, wearing a top hat and driven by a coachman with two horses, rolled through the streets of Cairo. The whole town turned out to see him.

The two biggest men around town then were a banker by the name of Stafford and a Mr. Halliday, speculator, hotel owner, steamboat builder. He was most cordial to the actresses and singers who came to town to appear at the Cairo Opera House; Maude Adams was one of them. The Opera House chandeliers now glitter upstairs in the Cairo Library.

Traveling the length of the Ohio between Marietta and Cairo, there was a figure I could not forget, and another almost audible sound. I kept thinking of General George Rogers Clark, the old Indian fighter. He put on war paint, like any savage, before some of his battles; and he danced his own war dance and came back from the fight with Indian scalps in his belt. In those days, there was an eerie light by night, the light of burning cabins the Indians had set ablaze. I thought of Clark, his Western campaign beginning, shooting the falls as the sun slipped behind the moon, and the earth darkened over the American wilderness. There were Indians who thought, as the darkness fell, their number was up and said so. And they were right. And I thought of Clark in his old age, living alone and bitter; then I thought of him facing the amputation of the leg he'd burned, calling for his old fifer and drummer. He set them to marching and playing around and around his cabin as the knife cut in, and there was only his jug to deaden the pain. But tough as ever, he got the job done; and it's the fife and drum that are there, just the other side of a thin sleeve of shadow beyond the trees, across the river, as you roll down the long valley of the Ohio.

## PART THREE

## The White Towns of the Prairies

Last summer, in a season of intense heat, Jim Burden and I happened to be crossing Iowa on the same train. He and I are old friends, we grew up together in the same Nebraska town, and we had a great deal to say to each other. While the train flashed through never-ending miles of ripe wheat, by country towns and bright-flowered pastures and oak groves wilting in the sun, we sat in the observation car, where the woodwork was hot to the touch and red dust lay deep over everything. The dust and heat, the burning wind, reminded us of many things. We were talking about what it is like to spend one's childhood in little towns like these, buried in wheat and corn, under stimulating extremes of climate: burning summers when the world lies green and billowy beneath a brilliant sky, when one is fairly stifled in vegetation, in the colour and smell of strong weeds and heavy harvests; blustery winters with little snow, when the whole country is stripped bare and grey as sheet-iron. We agreed that no one who had not grown up in a little prairie town could know anything about it. It was a kind of freemasonry, we said.

—WILLA CATHER
*My Antonia*

# 9

# NORTH
# TO IOWA

*Early years of settlement. The Amana colonies.*
*Tama, Iowa. A small-town cattle auction.*

In 1794, Able Sherman was dead. Pioneering folks from the East, flocking the wilderness trail, were launching off down the Ohio for the Western frontier. Ten years *before* he went to look for his cow, 12,000 made the trip, and he might well have been one of them Three years later, the number had jumped to 30,000 Ten years after his duel at the apple trees, the Louisiana Territory changed hands, and the Western frontier was ready to move beyond the Mississippi. That year buffalo robes sold for six dollars apiece; a bearskin went for three.

In 1825, the steamboats on the Ohio were jammed with people looking for adventure and home sites During the 40s, they went thronging into Iowa. And by the time the population was ready to move on west of the Mississippi, it was only 1850; that was the last year the buffalo came as far east on the prairies as Missouri's Ozark Highlands.

First the settlements appeared west of the Mississippi and then the road builders went to work to connect them. Often the people who built those roads, in one road district after another, were people working out their poll tax. That meant, as a rule, two days of work with a shovel; or if they could provide a team of horses and wagon, a roller or a scraper, one day. There was a general tax in addition to this which could also be worked out on the road gang.

The early roads were made with field rollers that were usually heavy logs of peeled sycamore. The roads cut straight off across the country, keeping between farms. The surface was level and drainage difficult. Such roads were in good condition about four months of the year; though sledding in the winter made transportation possible by other means than wagon.

The towns that developed along those roads were the ones Sherwood Anderson had in mind when he wrote: "In the days before the coming of industry, before the time of the mad awakening, the towns of the Middle West were sleepy places devoted to the practice of old trades, to agriculture and to merchandising. In the morning the men of the towns went forth to work in the fields or to the practice of the trade of carpentry, horse-shoeing, wagon making, harness repairing, and the making of shoes and clothing. They read books and believed in a God born in the brains of men who came out of a civilization much like their own. On the farms and in the houses in the towns, the men and women worked together toward the same ends in life. They lived in small frame houses set on the plains like boxes, but very substantially built. The carpenter who built a farmer's house differentiated it from the barn by putting what he called scroll work up under the eaves and by building at the front a porch with carved posts. After one of the poor little houses had been lived in for a long time, after children had been born and men had died, after men and women had suffered and had moments of joy together in the tiny rooms under the low roofs, a subtle change took place. The houses became beautiful in their old humanness. Each of the houses began vaguely to shadow forth the personality of the people who lived within its walls.

"In the farmhouses and in the houses on the side streets in the village, life awoke at dawn. Back of each of the houses there was a barn for the horses and cows, and sheds for pigs and chickens. At daylight a chorus of neighs, squeals and cries broke the silence. Boys and men came out of the houses. They stood in the open spaces before the barns and stretched their bodies like sleepy animals. The arms extended upward seemed to be supplicating the gods for fair days, and the fair days came. The men and boys went to a pump beside the house and washed their faces and hands in cold water. In the kitchens there was the smell and sound of cooking of food. The women also were astir. The men went into the barns to feed the animals and then hurried to the houses to be themselves fed. A continual grunting sound came from the sheds where pigs were eating corn, and over the houses a contented silence brooded.

"After the morning meal men and animals went together to the fields and to the doing of their tasks, and in the houses the women mended clothes, put fruit in cans against the coming of winter and talked of woman's affairs. On the streets of the towns on fair days lawyers, doctors, the officials of the county courts, and the merchants walked about in their shirt sleeves. The house painter went along with his ladder on his shoulder. In the stillness there would be heard the hammers of the carpenters building a new house for the son of a merchant who had married the daughter of a blacksmith. A sense of quiet growth awoke in sleeping minds. It was the time for art and beauty to awaken in the land."

And this, of course, was just what had set the Indians brooding.

We made our own crossing of the Mississippi into Missouri at Cape Girardeau and drove through town past intersections where baskets of artificial roses swung overhead. On our sixteenth day west, the following day, we reached the unpopulated, mountain forests of the Ozarks and turned north; and along that road we passed a man walking, wearing the high-crowned black hat of a mountaineer.

Rolling north through the Ozarks, the land began gradually to flatten and the next morning we went over the Big Muddy and into a region of typical Middle Western farmland. There were fences beside the road, fields of corn and livestock at pasture. And shortly, timeless town after timeless town rolled by: Moberly, La Plata . . . and crossing the Iowa border, Sigourney, North English, and Williamsburg with its brick streets, its homes with big lawns and a Mennonite woman we saw in the village square.

In a few more miles, we came to the Amana colonies. Seven in number, they're situated about twenty miles west of Iowa City and just off Route 6. They were settled by German mystics in 1855–65, though the society dates its founding to the year 1714. Their trail led all the way back across the hazy plains of history, past the old theosophist Jacob Bohme, all the way back to the fourteenth and fifteenth century and the time of Thomas A. Kempis and Johannes Tauler.

118

They had come to Iowa, looked around and bought up about 25,000 acres of the best prairie land they could find and then built villages of from forty to one hundred houses. The villages were modeled after the German *dorf* which placed the barns and sheds at one end of town and their factories and workshops at the other—with orchards, vineyards, gardens, and pastureland extending out on all sides.

Although Amana furniture, textiles, and other products have achieved an honorable place on the national market, the society saw itself in the beginning as a self-sustaining rather than a profit-making enterprise.

Their houses, still standing, rise two stories and are of brick or frame or brown sandstone; and some of the houses have trellises around their sides on which grapevines grow—the leaves shading and cooling the house through the summer months. Originally, there were no individual kitchens. There was a community kitchen instead, and a community dining room. The kitchens were big and notably clean. The families ate at long tables in the dining room, sitting on long benches with the men separated from the women and the children.

The colonists lived and fell in love and married and had families, but the single state was considered the most blessed. A married man, they figured, had to please his wife as well as God; and so if he stayed single he was freer to worship. There were, for instance, twenty-one rules by which the colonists were to live and Rule Eighteen was: "Fly from the society of woman-kind as much as possible, as a very highly dangerous magnet and magical fire."

The children of the colonies had even more rules. They had sixty-six! At school, they were to "show yourself kind and peaceable toward your fellow pupils, do not kick them, or make them dirty with your shoes or in some other manner; call them no bad names, and behave yourself toward them as you wish that they should behave towards you." Also: "In the wintertime do not go on the ice, do not throw snow balls at others, and do not go sliding with wicked boys." As if those rules weren't hard enough on a youngster, the next one read: "Take no pleasure in boisterousness and immodest plays; do not stand at the road when people quarrel or fight or do other knavery; never associate at all with licentious boys, for there you learn only wickedness; refrain also from playing with children of the opposite sex." There—you had that one again. And so it went.

A lot of the kids grew up and bolted the colonies, took up "worldly" ways; but they weren't read out of the society; nobody raged about it. The rebels met with "love and pity" and, in time, many returned. But in time, too, the colonies changed. They became more worldly. After the reorganization in 1932, the citizens of Amana, though religious still, were more like their neighboring "worldly" fellow citizens. Their kitchens are now serving people who drop in from the highway; and though the meals are served in the old-fashioned family style, the benches are gone and the tables are smaller.

We ate at the Ox Yoke Inn, a two-story house with an upstairs museum and a kitchen as immaculate and as shining as Amana tradition directed it to be.

Then it was only an hour's drive from the colonies to Tama. We were now in the heart of the land of lost roads and timeless towns of Mrs. H. Her grandparents were born in Iowa, some of her progenitors having been among the families moving down the wilderness trail, then along the Ohio toward the frontier. Tama was the home town—and a home town in which Sherwood Anderson would have felt comfortable.

Built on the banks of the Iowa River, Tama is bypassed by U.S. 30, and most of the passenger trains that used to stop now roll right on through. There are only two small industries, one a paper mill. And right in the town's backyard is a reservation of about six hundred Sac and Fox Indians.

Most, but not all, of the town's streets are paved; there are backyard and sideyard gardens; and backyard barns, grape arbors, and lilac bushes. Along the streets, the trees planted long ago have grown to a size to accommodate giants. Stumps can be found with floral decorations. White frame houses have lateral clapboard lines that show as dark, under the sunlight, as charcoal pencil strokes. The park is shaded and quiet around an old bandstand; and on the edge of the park, by the sidewalk, is a fountain with a dripping brim.

The main street of Tama, like so many of the small towns through which we'd passed, rested its foundations on the banks of an era when a sore throat was treated with a spoonful of coal oil and sugar, and men chewed Horseshoe plug-cut tobacco and smoked Duke's Mixture. Though dial phones were scheduled for installation, when we hit town the townsfolk still rang the operator to place their call.

Tama's older neighbor town is Toledo, but they look so similar and are so close to one another that they are more like a single than two separate villages.

My father-in-law seemed to be of the giants the trees of the town accommodated. He was big enough. He was a cattleman, a Chisholm type, although he'd been an Iowa farmer as well as a ranch foreman in Montana before he opened his own stockyard. He'd spent years in the saddle, and he walked with a slight roll that came not from long days and nights on the range but, incongruously, from an old football injury in college.

His stockyard was down along a railroad siding. The pens were empty now. Steers wouldn't be coming in for the market in any numbers until August and September, he said. Things were slow. The hog market, in fact, was at a forty-months' low.

When we drove down to the yards, there wasn't much to see because it was empty, ghostly, and quiet: penned-in areas of torn earth. Gates swung behind us. "I figure I better run some water in the troughs," he said. "About time." When they weren't used, he explained, the wood shrank and the troughs leaked. So he came down to the empty corrals and filled them now and then with water.

We crossed the ground to the railings on the far side. A strip of weeds grew up close to the railings. He leaned, and one huge hand went down into the weeds where the valve was hidden. When we left, the troughs were filled and reflected a cloudless sky. In a state that fattened hogs and cattle from the Western range on the grain it grew, and its grass, farmers and stockmen were watching the market, putting thoughts to the weather. The stockyard was ghostly not only with the cattle that had been and gone, but ghostly with the cattle to come and with troughs of water as well, over which only the air passed rippling the sky it reflected.

But there was some buying and selling each week. Something was always going on. Saturday morning, my father-in-law said, "Come on. Let's go see what's up," and we drove down to the auction yard.

Before we went inside, he said he wanted to take a look around and see what stock they were offering. He was curious

# INTO NEW MEXICO

HIGHWAY 64, NEW MEXICO

"The Taos Indian Pueblo is centuries old, and so are most of its customs."

"They still bake their bread in outdoor ovens, and they still use storage platforms made of pole flooring and upright supports."

TAOS INDIAN PUEBLO

"... the road divides around a historic adobe church."

RANCHES OF TAOS, NEW MEXICO

NEAR PENASCO, NEW MEXICO

"Following the road . . . we drove . . . across a countryside that's still Spanish New World in appearance and manner after four centuries."

LAS TRAMPAS, NEW MEXICO

"In the middle of town, we slowed down and stopped for a flock of sheep being driven across the street."

SANTA FE, NEW MEXICO

"resisting time and change in a setting that runs back for centuries through an American-Spanish-Indian past. The 'Anglos' are still in the minority."

TAOS INDIANS

Indians: ". . . by far the greatest portion still retain most of their aboriginal costume . . . the moccasin is the only part of the prairie suit that appears common to them all, and of both sexes . . ."—Joshua Gregg.

"... they generally wear their hair long—commonly fashioned into a queue, wrapped with some colored stuff ...."—Joshua Gregg.

TAOS INDIANS

CERRILLOS, NEW MEXICO

"The ageless Spanish and Indian towns of New Mexico extend out from Santa Fe, beaded along the roads in all directions."

about what sort of prices the cattle were going to bring; there was nothing he wanted to buy.

He climbed a railing ahead of me, and I followed. We walked on across the corral and a couple of lean Holstein cows, with metal tags in their ears, slid by. They were rolling their eyes, and they were worried. A man in overalls, carrying a whip, drove them on ahead.

On each side, there were stalls with plank railings and behind the railings, pigs as well as cattle. Most of the cattle looked as if they were either well-fattened or being fattened. We went down the aisle and at the far end leaned against the top railing and looked inside at some small fat yearlings that were, I was told, about the size the local butchers in the area liked. Their sides were sausage-round. They seemed gentle, and even as pampered as a couple of overfed pets.

It was the local butchers who probably supplied Lloyd's Restaurant in nearby Marshalltown. Lloyd's was more modern than the Ox Yoke Inn of the Amana colonies. But price, food, and surroundings considered, Lloyd's may be the best restaurant in the corn belt. Being in beef-fattening country, its meals were excellent, its prices low, and I felt guilty facing those fat, docile steers.

After a look, we went back to the shed where the auction was under way and we climbed up in among the tiers of seats around the small arena. There was an auction every Saturday. The auction yard and the ring below and the walls around had been standing for thirty years.

The auctioneer was chanting from behind a railed platform. There was a steer in the arena and two men. One of the men wasn't much older than a boy. He had a long limber whip in his hands and he used it to keep the steer jogging around. The other man was trying to pep things up in the stands by yelling out, "She's a good one" . . . or, "Sound one." But he wasn't used to yelling and he was getting hoarse.

Most of the men in the stands, watching and listening, were wearing railroad engineer caps and were dressed in blue denim overalls. They were listening passively, leaning forward. The auctioneer, who'd been a minister before his auction days, kept a singsong going and part of it went *"Ding-ding-ding . . ."* which I took to mean he was getting ready to wrap up the sale. Often he raised both arms in front of his chest and closed his fingers into fists and tugged, as if he were pulling on lines, pulling in bids from those passive faces above him. And what kept crossing my mind was how many times had the same figures, if not the same faces, sat here in shrewd-eyed quiet, for how many years back, the same scene over and over, how many Saturdays after how many Saturdays?

"Sometimes the speculators get ahold of those steers," my father-in-law said, "and the steers learn to trot on and off the scales by the door and get to be like performers in a weekly show."

I said, "Do you think any of the cattle up from the Southwest ever figure out what's going on? I mean—they're rounded up gaunt and hungry and shipped up here and fed corn and turned out to big, deep pastures of grass and told go ahead, eat, be happy; but doesn't a flicker of suspicion ever cross their minds there might be a hitch to it all?"

"No," he said. "No. More than likely, it's the other way around. I think if the cattle on that Arizona range ever got a notion of what the grass was like up here, they'd raise the worst racket and row you ever heard to get to it."

That night in Lincoln, Iowa, between two old wooden frame

buildings and not far from an old-fashioned general store, we passed a sight that summed up most of what we'd seen since the trip began and were still to see as we went on. Lincoln is another timeless town. We were walking along its main street in the nighttime, and what we passed was a movie. The ticket-taker stood on the sidewalk. In between the buildings, his audience sat on kitchen chairs. They were watching a drama thrown over their heads and onto a screen that made a bright square in the darkness at the end of the clapboard canyon. And it was all like a crazy dream of dream people watching still another dream.

In the faces of the people in the chairs watching the movie was the same passive scrutiny that had been on the faces of the men at the auction. Except that the bright square of light in the night showed steers on land crowded with piñon trees, with rocky crags behind them and cowboys slowly riding around and around!

## 10

# KANSAS

*The hills of grazing steers. Beyond the clock towers and the wheatfields, there were Indians.*

In many of the small prairie towns that look the same as they have for fifty or a hundred years, change is sometimes only an absence of something or someone, like the man who used to take an old file all aglow from his fire and lay it against an anvil and hammer it into as good a butcher knife as anyone would want—and be relaxed and casual about it, too. The blacksmith was a hard-working man, one of the hardest, in an age when people liked work, and the more the better. It was usually true that good men were the hardest workers around, and blacksmiths, as a lot, bore that out. Men took pride in strenuous jobs accomplished; but like the smith, they seemed to work without strain.

In those days of the settling of the prairies, men and women lived on more personal and intimate terms with the things they used, and they often watched and guided their making. But if there was one man in whom most skills resided, it was the

self-sufficient farmer. The best of them were their own blacksmiths . . . and carpenters . . . and coopers, too. The pioneer
American farmer was one of the most supremely independent,
and among the most proud and regal men the earth has
ever known. Those old faces in tintypes that so many Americans have in their family albums pack conviction. God was
with them. They had no doubts about it. Why should they
doubt? They prospered and their communities grew.

Montour was a small timeless Iowa town out of that era,
and leaving Tama and heading west, we passed through a good
many more such towns all day, and the next, and the next—
and along the way, a timeless countryside. We had lunch at
a small park outside Indianola. Across the highway, a country
road ran off between deep fields toward a barn and farm, and
I found myself thinking: We're the bridge. I mean by that . . .
all of my generation. We might not remember the pioneer
days, but our grandparents did, and we remember their memory of it. We saw, in them, the edge of it; and we touch that
edge as well as the edge of the age just ahead. But we're all
of us, all generations, bridges touching the edge of some
earlier era—feeling the swell of time like a sea swell within
us, feeling the strange sea depths of time below, and the
frightful beauty and loneliness of eternity on every side.

We were heading then toward the Flint Hills, an uplift of
limestone formation that ran north and south from Nebraska
to Oklahoma. We'd chucked our plan for picking up the old
Santa Fe Trail and following it off toward Dodge City and
the Southwest. My father-in-law, who knew the sort of
towns and the sort of countryside we were looking for, had
said, "Why don't you go south across the western part of
Kansas? As far back as I can remember, that countryside

hasn't changed. But most of the rest of it"—his finger moved across the map—"is different now; Dodge City, Abilene . . . they've changed so much I hardly know them when I see them . . ." He was another man, like the colonel in Pennsylvania, on easy, intimate terms with the past. He touched the edge of a generation that had seen the West open, and I listened.

The Flint Hills section was a prairie land that had once been lush, grassy paradise for the seemingly innumerable buffalo herds of the West: 4,000,000 acres of wild grazing contentment. The grass that grew there shot up stalks higher than the buffalo, and when cattlemen rode in on horseback for a first look around, the grass grew higher than their heads. The cattlemen liked that.

So, in the 1880s, wide-eyed cattle with the dust of the Chisholm Trail on their eyelids stared and then set in on that grass, which also gave its name to the hills. The Flint, or the Blue Stem, Hills as they're also known, run in a belt from thirty to sixty miles in width, and it was down through this belt we were directed.

Cattle had fed and fattened in these hills from New Mexico as well as Texas. It took one cowpoke to manage every two hundred head of cattle on a drive, and in a good year there had been up to 400,000 steers engrossed in eating their way to Chicago. And at the end of such cattle drives into Kansas, cowboys, along with drifters with delicately filed hair triggers, made towns like Dodge City and Abilene famous.

We worked our way from Tama west along U.S. 30 and then south. Before we came to Kansas City, we turned west again and crossed the Missouri. We passed into Kansas— another "bloody land," but not so dark as Kentucky with forest —bloodied not by Indian battles but by slave holders and free-soilers with lead-loaded "Beecher's Bibles." That was in the days prior to the Civil War, of the angry eloquence of pro-slavery Stephen A. Douglas and Abolitionist Wendell Phillips, the man Thoreau admiringly called the Red Cross Knight.

At Wamego, we turned south on Route 99 and plunged down through the old, old town of Alma toward the Flint Hills. It was 6:15. In Alma, the milk cans were out on the sidewalk. It was a turn-of-the-century town with a number of stone buildings and unpaved streets. A nearly treeless range-land followed, where the cattle, grazing the blocky ridges on each side, were clipping the grass down to lawn-bite length. The few trees that were in sight grew in the valleys by the edge of a stream. The land looked, I thought, like Scottish hills and lay smooth and glaucous from horizon to horizon.

We had dinner at Lake Wabaunsee, in a small roadside park where there were windmills silhouetted against the sky as well as the black cut-out arrangement of grazing cattle on the tops of two hills.

When we reached Eskridge, Kansas, it was dusk. We pulled up on a side street at the edge of the town park. We took a walk and picked up a friend, a black and white fox terrier. At nine o'clock, all the stores in town were closed except for two small cafés on the main street. There was a ring around the moon. The dog trotted along beside us, turning where we turned. As we came back toward the main street, a big dog came out of the shadows and jumped him. They snarled and snapped awhile and then our pal caught up with us, favoring a front paw. He was nosing around a café door when he got it slammed in his face, having more trouble than life, or at least our friendship, seemed worth; but he stuck with us.

Back at the car when we turned in, he lay down outside in the grass. I woke up a couple of times and looked out. He was still there—a dog that was plainly loyal. Rain drove him off before morning. When we got up at a dawn hour, he was gone.

The weather served up rain and overcast for our 23rd day west. We took 99 toward Emporia which was about 36 miles ahead of us. This town has grown vastly since the days it was spoofed in the Garden City, Kansas, paper of July 10, 1879: "The *El Dorado Press* says that Emporia is getting to be one of the best towns in Kansas. They have a daily newspaper, nine whiskey saloons, three railroads, a church festival once a week, one street lamp, two drays, a democratic street sprinkler, and thirteen fellows in jail."

Shortly after we'd crossed the Kansas Turnpike, we turned off on a back road looking for the Lyon County State Park. And we found it, following out the back country roads and the signs nailed to fence posts—and came to a lake and a stone pavilion; and there, as the rain fell intermittently, we got stuck. In circling the pavilion, I plowed our way through a pool of rainwater, lost speed and failed on the incline that should have taken us back to the road. The back wheels spun on the wet clay. There were no other cars anywhere around. That was at 9 A.M.

Josiah Gregg, the early merchant of the Santa Fe Trail, was once stuck himself not so far from where we were—in 1831. He said, "A bridge over a quagmire is made in a few minutes, by cross-laying it with brush (willows are best, but even long grass is often employed as a substitute), and covering it with earth, across which a hundred wagons will often pass in safety."

The grass in the fields around us had been recently cut and it lay yellowing. Mrs. H. got behind the wheel and I started gathering grass. I shoved it under the wheels, and the wheels took it from one side and threw it back out the other. I fell down; got sprayed with grass and clay; took off my shoes and went to pushing again. Quagmires are probably easier to cross than wet clay; that's all I can figure. Mrs. H. got us out by 11:30; I know the grass was no help, nor was I.

Olpe, eleven miles to the south of Emporia, is a little town that's been cut off by the highway. In the middle of the town in the middle of a street, a big yellow dog was stretched out in a puddle of sunshine and dream. Folks in farm clothing, in blue denim, that is, were walking about and the town pump was in use; and off behind the town pump an enclosed wooden stairway ran up along the side of an old general store.

Something else, like the town pump and the enclosed outside staircase that hasn't entirely disappeared, and that's out of the early days of automobile touring is the hand-operated gas pump.

Before we reached Moline in southwest Kansas, we pulled in for gas at a country store beside one of those great tall pumps, and I got out and looked at it. The tank that held the gas was a round cylinder glass affair. It was empty and the side of the glass was marked like a measuring beaker. The man from the store, his hands on a lever, started pumping. The gas poured in and rose up the sides of the tank; and when he'd pumped it full, the gas ran down the hose and into the car.

The performance alone, said Mrs. H., was worth the price of the gas.

At Moline we found that all the genuinely old-time hotels haven't disappeared either. Moline is another timeless town. The hotel, built in the 1870s, is a white frame structure. The foundation is brick; and a brick sidewalk rims the place. Inside the front door there's an unostentatious lobby out of Kansas antiquity. Beyond the lobby, a walnut stairway leads to the rooms which are all on the second floor. The hallway between the rooms is wide, and the floor is covered with linoleum. The rooms probably look as they have for close to a hundred years now: metal frame beds, old furnishings. In one room, there was a ceiling fan. The beds were comfortable. And since there was no running water in the hotel in the 1870s, the rooms have no baths. It's necessary to slip on a bathrobe and walk down the hall for that sort of convenience. Single rooms were $1.75; double rooms, $2.50. Everything was clean and neat . . . though the carpets were not, as ordered by a Kansas statute that stood on the books for many years, plastered. "All carpets and equipment in offices and sleeping rooms of hotels in this state," ran the provocative command, "including walls and ceiling, must be well plastered and be kept in a clean and sanitary condition at all times."

Sometimes the humor, as well as the wording, of the Kansas frontier was more deliberate. The following item appeared in the *Globe-Republican* of Dodge City on January 6, 1893:

*NOTICE TO ALL WHOM IT MAY CONCERN:*
There will be an election of new officers on February 31, 1893, of the Hugging Society. Applications for membership will be received on the date named. Here is the scale

of prices and benefits: Girls under 16 are not in it; from 16 to 20, 50 cents; from 20 to 24, 75 cents; school marms, 12½ cents; another man's wife, $1.00; widows according to looks from 10 cents to $3.00; old maids, three cents or two for a nickel. Not any time limit. Preachers are not charged. Editors pay in advertising, but are not allowed to participate until everybody else is through and even then are not allowed to squeeze anybody but old maids and school marms.

West of Moline, we drove into a late-afternoon fog. Along the road, the reflecting black surface was ablaze with the cold fire of rainwater; while above us the sun, burning through, suffused the overcast with a silvery light.

As the sky cleared slightly, the land flattened out and the hills fell away behind us. Far ahead and far back across the black, plowed earth, white grain elevators—sometimes they were only simple wooden towers—rose above the plains like castles. Kansas was the state in which Dorothy had lived, the little girl who was blown to the mythical land of Oz. I doubt if she was blown out of the state because Oz didn't seem far off, the way things looked as we drove through the fuzzy haze.

Almost every town of any size in Kansas has at least one good eating place, often a bright clean diner where the food is good and the cost of a meal less than a dollar and a half. The trick is to drive around town looking for the place where the most cars are parked. Local women are apt to cook, and cake and pies to be homemade. One such place is Ed's Grill in Wellington, Kansas, where our two dinners came to $1.90. There's no better proof of the existence of a continuous past than what the buck is still worth today along the highways of Kansas.

We ate and spent the night in Wellington. It rained all that night and when we got up the next morning, our 24th day west, it was still raining. Kansas highways are strung with timeless villages: Cambridge, Burden, Milan, Attica. Near Attica, a ghostly hand waved to us as we passed—a white glove tied to the cross wires over the gate to a ranch.

Then, clearing a small rise of land at Medicine Lodge, Kansas, we saw the Southwest come into view: the earth, a brimstone-desert coloring was spotted with bushy, green foliage and the land rolled back on each side into unplowed distances. Against a far horizon, under a blue sky of low-flying clouds, was a long mountain ridge that, in outline, was broken and crumbled. It was 9:40 A.M.

Beside the road a sign read: IN OCTOBER 1867, KIOWA, COMANCHE, ARAPAHOE, APACHE AND CHEYENNE INDIANS SIGNED PEACE TREATIES WITH THE FEDERAL GOVERNMENT. 15,000 INDIANS CAMPED NEARBY DURING THE COUNCIL . . . WHILE THE TREATIES DID NOT BRING IMMEDIATE PEACE, THEY MADE POSSIBLE THE COMING OF THE RAILROADS AND EVENTUAL SETTLEMENT . . .

But a few miles or so farther on, the glimpse we had of the Southwest abruptly vanished like a mirage. The dark, plowed earth of wheat fields returned. It wasn't until the late afternoon that the Southwest landscape reappeared. This time it stuck with us.

# PART FOUR

## A World of Sky

The Sky was as full of motion and change as the desert beneath it was monotonous and still,—and there was so much sky, more than at sea, more than anywhere else in the world. The plain was there, under one's feet, but what one saw when one looked about was that brilliant blue world of stinging air and moving cloud. Even the mountains were mere ant-hills under it. Elsewhere the sky is the roof of the world; but here the earth was the floor of the sky. The landscape one longed for when one was far away, the thing all about one, the world one actually lived in, was the sky, the sky!

—WILLA CATHER
*Death Comes for the Archbishop*

11

# THE ROAD
# TO SANTA FE

*Disturbance in a cowpoke's town. Back roads through Old Spain's New World.*

We'd reached the arid, open spaces, and the flat but undulating land was like a gray-green ocean of earth on which the ridges over which we passed were like swells of sea water. There were no trees and the shadows of the clouds darkened great desert areas that became like patches of strange seaweed all around us. There were fences, four strands high and barbed, on each side of the road, but these were the only fences we could see. We might as well have been rolling across a space as void and limitless as the sky. Except for small clusters of brown cattle in the distance, nothing moved. The fence posts, shaded on their near sides, cast shadows that were as black as slots cut into the depths of the earth under us. There were just the cattle, a few bones of windmills against the sky, occasional sun-baked boards on far-away ranch buildings, and that was all. We felt as if we'd shrunk to a minute size—as though the distant boulders were pebbles and the sagebrush was a kind of moss through which we were creeping.

At Hugoton, we turned southwest on Route 56 and in about 35 miles we'd left Kansas and crossed the border into Oklahoma. All the way across Kansas, the land had been rising to meet the Rocky Mountains. At Boise City, Oklahoma, we felt the altitude. I had a sinus headache and when I got out of the car, my knees were weak.

We were on the fork of the old Santa Fe Trail now that crossed the Cimarron . . . and between the Arkansas River and Santa Fe, there are still traces of that trail cut into the earth within sight of the highway. Gregg said of the same stretch: "On our passage this time across the 'prairie ocean' which lay before us, we ran no risk of getting bewildered or lost, for there was now a plain wagon trail across the entire stretch of our route, from the Cimarron to the Arkansas River.

"This track, which has since remained permanent, was made in the year 1834. Owing to continuous rains during the passage of the caravan that year, a plain trail was then cut in the softened turf, on the most direct route across this arid desert, leaving the Arkansas about twenty miles above the 'Caches.' This has ever since been the regular route of the caravans . . ."

But when it wasn't wet on that old Santa Fe Trail (which was more often the case), the land was so high and dry that the wood of the wagon wheels shrank and the iron rims rolled off. That was in the days when Gregg first clopped along the trail in his Dearborn carriage and Major Riley guarded the merchants against the "children of the desert." Among those "children" were the Comanches.

138

They slit the tips of their ponies' ears to mark them. They were the fancy horsemen of the plains. With bow and arrow in their hands, they could, riding at a full gallop, lean low to either side and, out from under the pony's head, fire away—with accuracy.

We stopped for the night in Clayton—a genuine any-century cowboy's cattletown just across the New Mexico border. This part of New Mexico has, as my father-in-law said, some of the richest cattle-raising land in the United States. Downtown, the people walking along the sidewalks were wearing cowboy hats and shirts, jeans and boots.

All over the West, from the biggest to the smallest towns, traditional cowboy garb is getting more and more common—worn by businessmen, governors, shop owners, as well as ranch hands. It's getting hard to tell who's a working cowboy and who isn't any more. In Clayton, however, chances are it's a working cowboy just in from a ranch.

Mrs. H. said we needed saddle soap. We crossed the street toward a store with tooled leather saddles in its window. Way far back in the shop, a young man sat, his shoulders and his head bent. He was at work, and he went on working for a while, and then put the piece of leather down and, wiping his hands on the side of his pants, came forward. We bought the saddle soap and went outside again. The street lamps were lighted, but it was still early. Most of the stores along the main street were open. There were only a few strollers. The town was quiet, but I had a feeling at a later hour it could, and often did, bust wide open. Here and there the bars were getting cowboy business, but things were still quiet.

After dinner, we drove around looking for a place to pull up and spend the night. We kept crossing the main street, plunging through its lights and then probing back along dark side streets; driving at times over unpaved roadway with potholes, sometimes on paving, almost always in tree- and house-flanked darkness that had Mrs. H. apprehensive. I'd say, "How about here?" and she'd shake her head. The trouble was, we couldn't find a park and that was what we wanted. There didn't seem to be any.

"How's this?" I said. We were on a street as swept with darkness as the rest we'd seen, but it looked more properly residential—as if along here a respectability of house and lawn were maintained. Mrs. H. nodded.

She got in back to let down the table to make up the bed. She worked with the lights out so we'd attract as little curiosity and attention as possible. There was always the chance someone might look out of the window of one of the houses and wonder what we were up to if we left the lights on.

I took a stroll up the street while I waited. I stood on the dark corner and looked about. The lights in the houses all around were out, and the trees along the street were plumed, black shapes against the sky. At such times I always felt as if eyes were on us, that we were watched. Yet, there'd been no trouble since we'd put the shore of the Atlantic behind us some twenty-five days ago. Oh, once, parked behind a school in Little Hocking, Ohio, we'd had to move. About the time sleep arrived, a floodlight snapped on us. We'd then driven a few blocks away and parked on a slope beside a church. That was the only trouble we'd had. But each night about this time, we both felt apprehensive.

I walked back to the car and got in the rear and pulled the doors closed and turned the handles up. Before we'd left New York, someone or other had said, "Once you're past the Mississippi, you can pull over anywhere along the highway without the cops waking you up with a flashlight, but east of the Mississippi, you want to be careful where you park for the night." They thought areas where new homes were under construction were the best spots. Anyway, the last thing I did when we turned in was to make sure the envelope with my identification papers was where I could lay a hand on it.

I slipped the leather strap over the upright handles on the door and settled back. We hadn't picked such a bad place. The street lights weren't close enough to be bothersome; there weren't any strafing headlight beams because there wasn't any traffic. It was a good spot.

I was asleep when Mrs. H. shook me.

I couldn't hear anything, but she was up on one elbow and had her head over near the window listening. I said quietly, "What is it?"

"Two men," she whispered.

"Where?"

"Out there . . ." She pointed up toward the front of the car. "They've got guns."

I pulled a curtain back slightly and took a look. There were a couple of men and they had on Western hats. They were kneeling down looking at my license plate. When they stood up, it did look as if one of them had a .45 strapped around his hips; and I heard the other say to him, "What do you think they're doing?"

They started walking back along the side of the car. As they came up by our window, I said, talking through the curtain, and through the opening in the window, "We're just pulled up for the night."

They stopped. "Okay," I heard. And they wheeled and walked off across the street.

But that was actually the only time we were disturbed, by people at least, on the entire trip. It was like a sheriff's posse out looking for someone else. Because the West still has its sheriffs and sheriff's posse mounted on horses and wearing Wyatt Earp outfits; and the West still has its rustlers, too.

The next morning we branched off the old Santa Fe Trail and up into the Sangre de Cristo Mountains. At Eagle Nest, we stopped for a 25-pound block of ice. The ice came out of sawdust. There it hung between the iron fingers of the tongs, clotted with the packing that had kept it from melting since it had been cut. The storekeeper doused it with a pail of water. It had been years since I'd seen a block of ice come out of sawdust.

Then: Kit Carson's countryside, Taos, New Mexico— where viga beams jut out of the walls of adobe houses, casting dark, diagonal shadows, and where there are narrow streets and dusky Spanish and Indian faces. The Indians have store-bought blankets wrapped around their heads and cast back over their shoulders.

Their pueblo is a few miles outside of Taos, and it's centuries old; and so are most of their customs. For that matter, so are the rituals and customs of the great majority of the Indian villages in the Southwest. They've resisted absorption by both the white man and the twentieth century, and they're as firmly rooted in the past as the Amish. Their ceremonies and dances are religious in nature and though the white man may come around and watch, cameras are forbidden.

The Taos Indian Pueblo picks up a little change by charging an admission fee, but it's the only Southwest Indian village

I heard of that did. I suppose tourists began to overrun the place and they figured it wouldn't hurt to cash in on their popularity. But they still bake their bread in outdoor ovens, and they still use storage platforms made of pole flooring and upright supports. Some of the buildings are four and five stories high, and even though the ceilings are low, that's high for adobe.

There's a back road out of Taos that runs to the right of the main highway to Santa Fe through Ranchito and Los Cordovas and then swings back to join 64 again. This is Route 240. It connects with Ranches of Taos, and there the road divides around an historic adobe church. Following the road off to our right, we drove down a narrow village street and into and across a countryside that's still Spanish New World in appearance and manner after four centuries. Routes 3 and then 75 and 76 took us in and out of the Carson National Forest and wound on ahead of us through old towns of adobe houses perched on the tops and the slopes of mountains above green, irrigated valleys.

Coming into Trampas, we passed alongside a primitive, hollowed-out half of a log carrying a steady stream of irrigation water; in the middle of the town, we slowed down and stopped for a flock of sheep being driven along the street.

An old woman in a black shawl walked along the earth-brown street in Truchas. In Cordova, a man was out repairing the wall of his adobe house with earth that had probably come from his own yard. In most of the towns, horses were free to stroll through the village.

In Cundiyo, a lady left a blanket loom inside a small village store to come out and operate an old hand gas pump. Across

143

the road, a woman bent, dipped two pails into a stream and carried them back down a flight of steps to her home.

And so by way of the Rio Grande and the back road from Taos, we came to the desert mountain city settled by the Spanish in 1610 which gave its name to the trail—Santa Fe.

Josiah Gregg, the American merchant who traveled the trail in 1831, nine years after the first wagon out of Independence traveled its length, made note of aspects of Santa Fe that are still to be seen today.

"The materials generally used for building are . . . unburnt bricks . . . These bricks are called adobes, and every edifice, from the church to the palacio, is constructed of the same stuff . . . The roofs of the houses are all flat *azoteas* or terraces . . . The floors are constructed of beaten earth 'slicked over' with mortar, and covered generally with a coarse carpet of domestic manufacture . . .

"Among the least unpleasant customs of this country is that of the siesta or afternoon nap . . .

"Around Santa Fe, the word *pueblo* does not mean 'people' or even 'town' so much as it does a group or village of Indians who have been Christianized. They are, in short, a remarkably sober and industrious race, very little given to quarrelling or dissipation, except when they have had much familiar intercourse with the Hispano-Mexican population . . . Several of these Pueblos have been converted into Mexican villages . . .

"The dress of many of the Pueblos has become assimilated in some respects to that of the common Mexicans; but by far the greatest portion still retain most of their aboriginal costume . . . the moccasin is the only part of the prairie suit that appears common to them all, and of both sexes . . . they generally wear their hair long—commonly fashioned into a queue, wrapped with some colored stuff . . .

"The tortilla, the *atole,* the *piñole,* and *many* others, together with the use of *chili* are from the Indians."

And that's the way it still stood in Santa Fe when we found it nearly 130 years later: an unassimilated blend of cultures resisting time and change in a setting that runs back for centuries through an American-Spanish-Indian past. The edges overlap, but that's about all. And the "Anglos" are still in the minority.

Santa Fe and the countryside all around is loaded with restaurants and hotels which carry that atmosphere. To name just a few of the places: in Taos there's an adobe restaurant called La Doña Luz that serves exceptionally good food; and the owner-manager makes a yearly trip to France to stock up on wines. Entrees run from around $2.50 to $4.50.

In Santa Fe, there are a number of good inns—La Fonda Hotel has rooms furnished with furniture of many colors, beamed ceilings and tin-framed mirrors on the walls. A single room costs $6.50; a double $10. La Posada Inn is a motel that looks like an adobe village. Many of its rooms have beamed ceilings and fireplaces. The lobby is at the foot of the stairs of a house a hundred years old. Singles are $7.50; doubles from $9 to $12.

Among the restaurants in Santa Fe, we especially liked The Shed on Burro Alley. It's a place with brick floors, tables of thick, polished wood and a low, beamed ceiling. The food was excellent and the prices were moderate.

There are a couple of interesting restaurants south of town, one Spanish and the other out of Billy-the-Kid Western days. The Spanish restaurant, La Mancha, is in Galisteo on a ranch that's been in operation since 1593. Between the bar and the dining room, there's a path lighted with torches. The prices are reasonable.

The prices are also reasonable at a restaurant called Tiffany's in Cerrillos. It's on a corner, edged by an old wooden sidewalk with hitching posts in a town Western enough for a Hollywood set designer. The evening we came by, oil lamps were burning on the walls among stuffed eagles and owls and deer heads. You sat in the barroom, and the bar is *muy autentico*. For $1.95, you're entitled to all you can eat, and it would be hard to eat better for twice the price.

We'd been on our way west for thirty days when we left Santa Fe for the mountains and the mining towns of western Colorado. The ageless Spanish and Indian towns of New Mexico extended out from Santa Fe, beaded along the roads in all directions. We threaded our own string, moving north through tuftaffeta mountainsides of piñon and juniper trees: Abiquiu (another world, another time) and then Coyote, Gallina, Llaves, Vado, Tierra Amarilla . . .

In Tierra Amarilla, I walked down the street to the place called the "Poor People's Store" and went inside. A boy was sitting on the counter talking to two girls. They were all in their teens, all talking rapidly in Spanish. This was a place where the people in and around the town came for supplies. It was rudimentary—the way stores started out to be when sometimes there was only a wagon to carry the necessary items a settler or a farmer needed. There was a showcase, but there was little to show inside it. Behind the counter were shelves and on the shelves were rows of nationally advertised products, but the shelves weren't crammed with goods the way they are in the supermarkets. Here was a store where the customers'

146

# PAST COLORADO MOUNTAINS

NEAR OURAY, COLORADO, ALONG THE MILLION DOLLAR HIGHWAY

SILVERTON, COLORADO

"The slopes dropped down and down; . . . and then we came out of the heights into Silverton."

SILVERTON, COLORADO

"... one of Colorado's old boom towns ... Not much has changed."

The jailhouse.

SILVERTON, COLORADO

TELLURIDE, COLORADO

"It was a good-sized town before the end of the century, as Colorado towns went . . ."

TELLURIDE, COLORADO

"The opera house was closed."

TELLURIDE, COLORADO

". . . but just inside the door, time
flipped over like a coin or a page,
and it was long ago with the show
about to begin."

# ALONG DESERT ROADS

BEDROCK, COLORADO

ON THE ROAD TO DEAD HORSE POINT, UTAH

"Rain was falling; but now and then the sun came through and lit the landscape."

NATURAL BRIDGES NATIONAL MONUMENT, UTAH

Not a lost road, but a lost world.

BETWEEN BLANDING AND FRUITA, UTAH

"Route 95, between Blanding and Fruita, Utah, crosses what is some of the most remote, uninhabited canyon wilderness left in the United States."

"We drove on only a few more miles and pulled off on a hump of land above the river and at the top of a long dip in the road."

ROUTE 95, UTAH

ROUTE 95, UTAH

". . . the trapdoor in the floor of the canyon opened, and we dropped
back, back back—before memory even began . . ."

"The Mormon villages we saw . . . were more like our early pioneer settlements: rustic, unpaved farm villages . . ."

GRAFTON, UTAH

ANTIMONY, UTAH

"There were a couple of Mormon churches . . . The boards by the front steps had been burned black from a fire that almost got out of hand. There was a constant danger of fire . . ."

PIPE SPRINGS NATIONAL MONUMENT, ARIZONA

". . . we found a door typical of the region . . ."

"The window glass in the east wall was filmed with dust, too, and had bullet holes in it."

BETWEEN TEMPIUTE AND WARM SPRINGS, NEVADA, ALONG ROUTE 25

"The shack looked uninhabited and deserted."
BETWEEN TEMPIUTE AND WARM SPRINGS, NEVADA, ALONG ROUTE 25

"... Tonopah, Nevada, one of the famous old silver queens of the West
... half a billion dollars in ore ..."

GOLDFIELD, NEVADA

"Fire hit a lot of the town in 1923, and gutted the walls of an old saloon and gambling hall near the local school."

ON THE PORCH OF THE SANTA FE CLUB,
GOLDFIELD, NEVADA

"It was still like the old days, though things had come down a little, got worn and sometimes broken."

GOLDFIELD, NEVADA

The Word as applied to the frontier far to the west of Lancaster, Pennsylvania. The Bible was about the only book anyone read.

wants weren't expected to be too varied. And like the old-time village store, this was a place where the attitude of the clerk, and the attitudes of the customers, too, were relaxed and neighborly.

The two girls both laughed at something the boy said and then one of the girls replied and the boy laughed. He slid off the counter, went around behind it and came up to where I was standing. "You like something?"

The words were English, but that was all. They came out wrapped in Spanish vowels and consonants.

We drove on through similar towns: Park View, Brazos, Chama, all in the space of an easy day's drive from Santa Fe; all towns of adobe houses with long portals. There were wooden wells in front yards and in backyards, there were piles of kindling wood. There were horses in enclosures of pole fences, and in one front yard, a white horse was hitched and saddled, waiting for his rider. There were no sidewalks anywhere.

# 12

# MINING TOWNS OF
# THE SAN JUAN MOUNTAINS

*Silverton. Ouray. Telluride.*

Between Pagosa Springs and Durango, Colorado, Highway 160 passes Chimney Rock and then heads toward a length of cliff that looks as if it could be the edge of the world. Pine trees grow at the foot, at the edge of a fertile valley, and the road winds and turns along it.

We were in the mountains of Colorado that had received the prospectors, bouncing back from the California gold rush. Those mountain slopes and valleys saw their share of the great American treasure hunt; and Colorado mines were still running, the treasure still tumbling out.

We came to Durango. There were people on the streets in Western outfits. There were Indians too. By now, they were getting to be a common sight. North of Durango, the Million Dollar Highway (Route 550) began. That's a road that was surfaced with gravel high in gold content, and the million bucks refers to the richness of the gravel rather than the fat bill from the contractor.

A stream ran to the right of the road, the Rio de las Animas Perdidas, which got a thorough going-over by the placer miners in the 1860s. A bridge across the stream was named after a Captain Charles H. Baker who, with his party of nugget hunters, pitched the original span in 1861.

On our 32nd day west, we came into Silverton, Colorado, along a road with a drop-off to our right that backed the reputation of the San Juans as the highest bunch of mountains in the United States. The slopes dropped down and down; and we passed a green rincon with a ranch far below us; and then we came out of the heights into Silverton.

The road was steep and passed a mountainside of red, yellow, and green. Where the mountainside wasn't green with foliage, it seemed made of colored waxes that had melted in the sun and run together. Beyond that mountain, at the end of the drop in the road, was Silverton.

Silverton is one of Colorado's old boom towns. It's not a ghost town, but a lot of its old houses stand empty. Not much has changed. The streets, most of them, are still unpaved. There aren't any parking meters. And inside one of the town's drugstores, I noticed that the linoleum had, in places, worn through to the boards of the floor. Although Silverton is a "found" timeless town insofar as the local merchants and the visitors are concerned, the place hasn't been prettied up. It's being preserved.

A narrow gauge railroad, one of the few left in the country, runs between Durango and Silverton, bringing in tourists with each run—and staging for those tourists a running gunfight up the middle of a dirt street to the wooden sidewalks in front of the old Bent Elbow Saloon.

The town hotel, the Grand Imperial, had been restored; a

149

quarter of a million dollars had gone into the restoration which, in cases like this, is as much a labor of love as it is of profit. The hotel had a mahogany-back bar, circa 1882, big plate-glass mirrors from Paris, and all in all, it was a mountain mining-town inn open for service with the years rolled back. Rates for single rooms started at $4; doubles at $8.

There's been an interest in restoring old hotels in American small towns that's been under way now for some time, and it's spreading. In Durango, the Strater Hotel was getting the finishing touches on a face-lifting that returned the place to her elegant days of Victorian red plush, marble, and high polish.

In Ouray, however, twenty-three miles above Silverton, the Beaumont Hotel might, to some travelers, be even more atmospheric because it's less restored than it is well-preserved. It has many of its original furnishings. On the second floor, the dining room is wood-paneled with a high ceiling; Madame Luisa Tetrazzini once sang from a balcony over the dining room. The clock at the landing has been stroking off what would seem to be the nonexistent hours since the hotel opened. The stair well is three stories high, with white railings; a chandelier hangs from the skylight. In our room, No. 3, we found a black and rose floral carpet, walnut bed, coat tree, marble-topped dresser with a mirror, and a marble washbasin in one corner. Reasonable rates.

The road that goes to Ouray from Silverton runs on through the San Juan Mountains along Route 550. Not so far past an old abandoned mine along the side of a steep slope, an astonishingly deep-set town appears. Traveling that length of road is like a flying dream. Down you swoop.

Ouray isn't just cupped by mountains—it seems deeper than that; so deep it's at the bottom of a well formed by the sides of the surrounding rock. In the winter, we were told, the snow falls straight down the hollow of the well to the housetops with hardly a flutter.

That night when we took a walk around the town, if there was a moon shining, none of its light came over the edge of the mountain rims far above us, and those faceless black mountains loomed like the pit walls of the dark eternity out of which the mountain mining towns of America so suddenly appeared, and to which they so soon returned.

It was ten o'clock when we came back to the main street and stood looking down the length of it. Ten o'clock—and I could count only eight lighted signs.

The next morning we took Highway 550 north for another ten miles and then swung off on Route 62 and headed west for Placerville and the turn to Telluride. There were fewer of the craggy mountains. The land became more like a wilderness. A stream turned up beside the road; and within half a mile of one another, we saw a porcupine and a beaver.

The turn at the San Miguel River led us toward Telluride. Just past Placerville, we stopped and got out and crossed the river on a wooden footbridge to fill our vacuum bottles. It was then fifteen miles to Telluride, an old mining town that's changed less since its wild and wide-open days than any we saw.

At the end of town where the mountains narrow and join is a mine still in operation and beside the mine, the usual tailings pond—a tombstone gray dune of fine sand and residue. Rippling through the town itself, from the stream out of which so much gold came, is the sound of water running over stones.

It was in 1875 that the first gold strikes got going, and the founding of Telluride followed in 1887. It was a good-sized town before the end of the century, as Colorado towns went: it had an elegant hotel and an opera house.

The opera house was closed. The small marquee above the entrance had seven colored bulbs, three of which were broken down to their sockets. It hadn't shown a movie in ten years; but just inside the door, time flipped over like a coin or a page, and it was long ago with the show about to begin.

At the top of a flight of stairs was a ticket window flanked by a couple of posters that dated dack to the days of the melodrama. And so did the theater and the stage and the painted curtain. Behind the stage, a door opened into Room 18 of the Sheridan Hotel.

There is a picture of the hotel taken years back on one of the town's big days. In front of the hotel is a speaker's platform; above the platform, at the windows of the hotel, people are gazing out over the street—everyone a woman. In those days, Telluride ran wide-open around and around the clock.

The women are no longer at the windows, the streets are quiet, but it's a Telluride that's timeless. And it seems to be an undiscovered town at that. A walk along any of its streets is a walk in another century. Even on the main street, grass sprouts from the curbs, and a dog slept on the sidewalk under a *WELCOME TO COLORADO* sign. There didn't seem to be any tourist business. There the town is, sort of pristine in its crumbling beauty and lost, far lost, in the past.

So are the lobby and the bar of the Sheridan Hotel. They're virtual time capsules; even the air in the lobby seems sealed in. Old hotel registers and records are strewn about on a table for inspection. There are rock specimens, leather chairs, brass spittoons, and doors with stained glass. The lobby and bar are connected by a number of curious and vaguely sinister rooms. This, like all of Telluride, is for the purist time traveler.

As we left Telluride, the sky was overcast. It had rained briefly and then stopped. We passed a field of sheep on our left grazing over the wet grass. The San Miguel Canyon and River came up; the mountainside above us was red. Pine trees grew down the mountain all the way to the stream and the stream bottom of round boulders; and along where the water was flowing swiftly, leaving white streaks of froth, hardwood trees grew. They sent up slim trunks that carried a foliage of light, bright green.

The road followed along the side of the river, some fifty feet above it and cut into the canyon's side: a winding road through a colorful gorge. The road back to 550 gave us the morning's scenery in reverse. We passed a mountainside that came down to the road in a steplike formation, and the pine trees that stood on the steps were like strange creatures, not so much of another planet, but of an inner world.

A little later we descended, with the road, toward the floor of a valley the size of a great crater. This valley was green and fertile—a cloud-shaded, virtually uninhabited region: here and there a few ranches, now and then a passing car, and that was all.

As we came in view of Route 550 again, the ridges of the mountains set against the far horizon to the east looked like the skyline of a fabulous city of palaces and temples.

We spent the night beside the Black Canyon. I thought of the Gunnison River cutting through the canyon walls half a mile below us. I thought of the Gunnison and of the Colorado and of the Rio Grande running through the darkness and on across the western wastes of America—all in utter, seemingly endless solitude. I thought of the night wind in the piñon and the juniper in the desert—and no one to hear it, or to see the rock and brush in the moonlight. I thought of these places, empty, beautiful, and unwitnessed long before I'd been born— and remaining unchanged, living on, long after I'd be gone.

What a world—so strange, streaming along on time through the universe. I felt like a tourist from outer space who had managed by the simple trick of birth to reach this planet for a visit. It seemed pointless to yearn for a rocket trip to Mars or to a world around another star.

## 13

# BELOW

# AND BEYOND TIME

*The stone from the sea behind us. The lost world of Dead Horse Point. Into Utah canyon wilderness.*

In the morning we drove back to Montrose, Colorado. We picked up Route 90 and headed west. It was ranch country and irrigated. We crossed a small bridge and I pulled the Camper up on the other side by the banks of a deep, swift stream no more than ten yards wide. Its banks were high and grassy. Small, gray birds were already at breakfast. There were about thirty-five in the flock and they were busy diving on the insects swarming just above the water. They came diving down, skimmed the surface and then rose.

The sun had been up only a little while. We could see the sunlight reflecting brightly from the insects. The birds dove through them, wings rigid; and then, wings aflutter, shot up and circled for another run. They came skimming in so low that sometimes their breast feathers broke the opaque, green flow.

As we sat there, the radio reported rainstorms over the

Western United States. The radio reported heat as well; but where we were, it was cool and pleasant and sunny. Not far away, behind a rail fence, three horses were grazing by a shed of cypress logs. In the far distance, purple with haze, were the jagged mountains through which we'd passed yesterday.

West on Route 90: miles of rail fence, five rails high, zig-zagging beside the gravel road; the road rose steadily. There aren't many rail fences left any more, though once fences like those had been abundant enough. When the early roads had begun to tie settlement to settlement, farms had to be fenced in. With trees and wood plentiful, rail fences, also known as worm and snake fences, appeared. Instead of being five rails high, they were eight, as a rule, and stood anywhere from four and a half to six and a half feet in height. The bottom rails rested at the corners on short, hardwood sleepers and the rails, like the ones beside the road on Route 90, were some ten feet in length, slanting in about four feet before they angled out again. A good fence, when finished, was always hog-tight, bull-strong, and horse-high.

We came to the Uncompahgre National Forest, and then the Uncompahgre Plateau. This was a forest area through which cattle ranged. At lunchtime we drove off the road in among a clump of pine trees. The ground was matted with fallen needles and cones.

It was at this spot, sorting around among the cans and bottles on the cabinet shelves, that I came across a small, round white stone I didn't know what to make of, or how to account for. It wasn't anything I'd put there. I held it up and asked Mrs. H. what it was.

She was sitting at the table, spreading bread. "That's mine," she said and went right on spreading bread with only the briefest glance. I was outside at the back of the Camper with the door up. I handed her the bottle of olives. She took it and I said, "How long has that been in there?"

"Since New Jersey," she said blithely.

"Since where in New Jersey?" I said slowly.

"Since Atlantic Highlands. I picked it up on the beach."

"Cut it out."

"What do you mean, cut it out?"

"Are you telling me you actually picked it up that first morning, the morning I waded out to fill that pop bottle?"

"I did."

"I didn't see you."

"I did though," she said, and opened the olive bottle and began to fork them out. But she must have seen how ecstatic I looked because she said suspiciously, "Why?"

"Because now I've got something from the Atlantic to throw in the Pacific. I thought I didn't have anything."

"I don't want that thrown in the Pacific. That's mine."

"It'll make a beginning and an end," I said.

"It's a keepsake!"

That's a woman for you. They just don't understand the grand gesture.

"Did you really pick it up on the beach?"

She let me have her stern, level gaze and said, "Do you think I'd tell you I had if I hadn't?"

No—I didn't. I put the stone back in a corner where I'd be sure of finding it again. It had probably soaked in the ocean water I'd lost I told myself.

And so, consequently, lunch was more of a joy than usual. Driving on, after lunch, coming down from the plateau, the land became more arid. It got more like the Western landscape

I was familiar with through Western movies. There was no traffic. The gravel road where we were traveling was, of course, important in suggesting that cowboy-Western rangeland setting. It was the type of road on which a stagecoach might more naturally turn up around the bend ahead than a car or a truck.

Far below, on our right, a stream appeared. The road wound along above it. And then, turning with the road away from the river, rounding a bend, we saw a ranch and beside the ranch house, log sheds. A horse was saddled and waiting near the house. But there were no people moving anywhere. There was only this nineteenth-century Western setting, complete in every detail, like a diorama, as we drove by.

Outside Naturita, we picked up Highway 46 and continued west 36 miles before we came to the Utah border. The road was blacktop now and, on each side, grass grew a luminous green, so bright it seemed to light the roadway for miles ahead; and on the right and on the left, the earth swept back, flat, to high cliffs; and down, down, down a slot in the earth we went, down a chute toward a town called Paradox; and there, twenty-five miles from Naturita, the road took its first bend. We swung up a long curve along a mountainside and dropped into a second canyon where the road curved along a mountainside and dropped into still another canyon and curved away among eroded rocks and hills of shale and sandstone.

We crossed the border, turned left on Utah 160—and just outside Moab, deep in Zane Grey's canyon cliff country, we ran into a storm. The air was red with whirling dust, the sky overcast. I pulled the car off the road and in close to a building until the worst of the storm had blown itself out.

Eleven miles north of Moab, we turned left on the road to

Dead Horse Point. Rain was falling; but now and then the sun came through and lit the landscape with a xanthic glow. The road got worse as we went along. It was a good many rough miles in from the highway, across desert desolation, before we reached, at dusk, the rim of the canyon lookout. And there, with what seemed a world to ourselves, we decided to put up for the night.

This, I figured, was the plaza to the city that sometimes seemed to take shape in the sides of the cliffs beside the road —this was what lay behind the battlements and towers. It was a city like Atlantis, some long-gone kingdom. We stood looking out over a vast sea of air and earth: a sunken world where a river flowed narrowly, the river made infinitesimal by its own carving. The river was the Colorado. Its banks were green, the water an olive drab, flowing 3000 feet below; eternal stone, eternal sea. And there we were, utterly alone, no house, no sign of any other single living, moving thing.

There are dinosaur tracks in Utah's canyon rocks; standing where we were, I don't think I'd have had to see one to believe we were back among them in that state where, in fact, Indian petroglyphs of the mastodon actually exist. Some authorities say that 15,000 years passed between the extinction of the mastodon and the appearance of man on earth. Nevertheless, at Hys Bottom along the Colorado and not so far from where we were standing, there are pictures of the mastodon drawn in stone.

In New York before the trip West had started, I'd thought the beginning of our trip would drop us a long way back into the past. The Eastern part of the United States, standing as it does deeper in our own history than the rest of the country, would start us out, I figured, somewhere in the seventeenth or eighteenth century; and then I saw the roads West, rising gradually up the slope of time to our present century. But it hadn't been so. The mistake I made was a common one. I was imagining early America as an uninhabited wilderness except for the colonies on the Eastern seaboard. We've barely brushed away the dust over the history of the people of this land of ours; and I was forgetting such recent inhabitants as the French and the Spanish—and the Aztecs too. I'd forgotten the Orient was here ahead of us.

Anyway, I was wrong; the valleys of time hummock and drop from era to era, and the road West wasn't a gradual rise. Beginning in New Mexico and finally in Utah, we felt the bottom drop out of sight.

Route 95, between Blanding, and Fruita, crosses what is some of the most remote, uninhabited canyon wilderness left in the United States crossed by any kind of road at all. It's trail road; and warnings are up to carry water.

Twenty-four miles south of Monticello, Utah, we made our turn west on 95. It was 1:40 in the afternoon. Then, just beyond the Natural Bridges National Monument, we found ourselves on the bottom of a canyon like the one we looked down into at Dead Horse Point. We were on the floor not of a lost road, but of a lost world; led there, as a matter of fact, along the old Spanish Trail that lay between Moab and Monticello.

The earth was reddish and the desert brush and trees beside the road were, under the dust, like a roseate fungus. Flanked by canyon walls on each side, we drove by the edge of a white canyon sunk in the earth; a canyon within a canyon, white within red. Down between high red walls we went, slowly, all afternoon. Five hours: 75 miles. The canyon shadows moved across the earth like a tide. Up ahead the canyon ended, walls joining, and we made a sharp turn around the sunken point of the white canyon and back along the inner canyon's far side; and then off up a side canyon, turning with the winding road.

Within twenty minutes, the sun no longer slanted down over the high canyon walls, and it was dusky. Then, over some six miles of rough road, we reached the tiny settlement of White Canyon. By that time, the walls of rock had closed in on each side and we were driving along an alleyway of cliffs. There was, at White Canyon, appropriately, a service station for "gas, welding, and repairs."

Just beyond White Canyon, the road came to an end at the bottom of a cliff and at the turbulent edge of the Colorado. Overhead, and cut into the cliffs, I learned sometime later, there were ancient Indian dwellings; but I didn't see them then. I just stood staring at the water and then over across the way.

A thick cable looped over the river to the far shore where a small ferry was moored. Over there the road continued, went on and up an incline where I could see a small house against the sky. I wasn't sure if anyone in the house kept an eye out for cars or not, and I stood looking at it for quite a while. Nothing happened. I finally turned and walked back along the road under the cliff until I came to a phone I'd seen. The wires were gone, and it was dead. I walked on back to the car again . . .

In the 1870s, a man, generally classified with the renegades of his time, had set himself to the job of washing "flour gold" from the sandbars in the vicinity. He'd named the place "Dandy Crossing." It was one of the Colorado's four most natural crossings, and the Indians had been using it for a long time. Now the crossing was used by uranium prospectors. But I'd about given up getting us across that evening, when a man appeared.

He came walking down the long, sloping road on the other bank, bare from the waist up, wearing a sun helmet. A small dog trotted along beside him, a black cocker spaniel. It didn't take him long to reach us.

The ferry was a floating platform on pontoons with side railings, driven back and forth along the cable by a kind of amphibious tractor mounted to one side. When it reached our shore, I drove down and out between the platform railings. Our wheels were blocked; we got out.

In times when the current of the river was flowing swiftly, the man in the sun helmet said the river moved along at 15 feet a second. The water looked fast then, but he said it was relatively low.

"Cable ever break?" I asked.

"Not yet," he said.

"Get much traffic through here?"

I could lean on the railing and talk to him. He sat in the pilot's seat a few feet away. "You're the only folks been by today," he said.

I looked back where the rusted hulk of an old car lay with its nose like an alligator up on the bank, the river flowing around it. Its front wheels were gone, its windows too.

"What happened to the car?"

"Some folks having a little party; brake slipped . . ."

"They all get out?"

"Yeah."

"What happened to the wheels?"

He laughed, "Can't leave a car alone long around this part of the country and expect much to be left on it."

It was good and hot then, late in the day though it was. When we reached the far bank, he got in the car with us and we drove up to his house. Then he and I got out and went inside where he wrote out my receipt. The fare, with tax, was $5.50.

It was a little cooler, but not much, at the house which was in among river-bank trees. It wasn't the one I'd seen from the bank on the far side. He had cabins, he said, which he rented to people who wanted to stay overnight; but we were moving on.

When I signed the register, a drop of my sweat fell to the page. I asked him how he kept cool way out here in a nowhere with the sun rifling its rays down, and he just grinned and said, "You can't." He stood there in his sun helmet, a pleasant-looking man with sharp blue eyes, his face tanned and moist. At least the house, with the blanket-covered chairs all around, was shaded. But he didn't seem to mind the heat. And then I knew what it was about the tanned, bare-chested man and the isolation of rock and sky at the river's edge that I was reminded of. For an instant, standing in that heat, I wondered if by any chance we had just crossed the River Styx. I think that today Charon himself probably wears a sun helmet, runs a diesel ferry and has the same pleasant, patient smile for all his passengers. Anyway, I don't think it was the River Styx, but one never knows, even now.

Beyond Hite, the road hugged the bottom of a cliff; was no more than a ledge above the muddy Colorado. It was getting darker. We drove on only a few more miles and pulled off on a hump of land above the river and at the top of a long dip in the road.

We had traveled all afternoon through heat and isolation. It was a warm night; but the river looked too deep and too fast for swimming. About midnight, the sky clouded over and rain fell. I woke up when I felt the rain on my face and closed the door in the roof of the Camper. When the sun rose in the morning, the sky was clear again and the day, for a time at least, was cool.

It was, as I said, in New Mexico and in Utah that the bottom dropped out of time. To be precise, it was just beyond Hite and the Colorado River that the trapdoor in the floor of the canyon opened, and we dropped back, back, back—before memory even began; all the way back to the petrified jungles of the Id.

After breakfast, we drove slowly down between red canyon walls. We were only halfway to Fruita, with another sun-glazed day coming up. The road was rock and sand, but it was firm and we moved along between walls that seemed like marble, or rather that varied between walls as smooth as red marble and red walls as pitted as bug-riddled wood. And there were trees with rough gray bark and spade-shaped leaves growing in the loose sand among sagebrush, rabbit brush, and snake grass. And then we found ourselves in Tartarian pockets of the road where the rocks began to take on the shape of grief-dreary gods. There was a lion-headed monster around one bend, and a little farther on, a limbo-mama with the head of a hound, her eyes closed and her cluster of pups gathered about.

And then—red walls gone, there were blobs of rocks, smooth, solid, plantless, and mountain-sized, as if some giant with his head among the stars, a primordial Picasso, had passed along this way making shapes for dreams. I mean by that, when I looked at them, I felt the shape of them, and the size of them, too. I felt them solidly inside me, but when I tried to pick them back out, they were no larger than the size of a grapeseed, and they weighed tons and tons.

Then, beyond those round, brown, billowing rocks, the road turned toward distant mountains that were green. The canyons were gone. Now: desert country, sagebrush and shifting, wrinkling sand. The ground became more solid; the desert opened out wider and wider on all sides. Just before noon, we came to Hanksville—and then, beyond Hanksville, we came to the Mormon women.

**14**

PIONEER
UTAH VILLAGES

*The stranded Mormon women. Menace at
Capitol Reef Gorge. Of hidden towns and plural
marriages.*

Hanksville, in the 1880s and '90s, was a meeting place for the
outlaw gangs in the region. These were gangs that had a good-
enough hold on the territory to the east and to the west to be
tolerated in the few small settlements around—even welcomed. The biggest and probably most welcomed of the lot
was the Robber's Roost Gang: cattle rustlers, every last one of
them.

Today Hanksville has a population somewhere around 50;
does a little mining and some farming; and has a couple of
gas stations as well as a general store.

Beyond Hanksville we entered a lifeless-looking landscape
of bentonite that had been carved and shaped by the rain and
the wind: gray forms, rounded and duned. Then, about halfway to Capitol Reef National Monument, rolling along over
desert "trail," we came across two cars stopped on the road.

A man in sunglasses, a blonde, and two stout women in

166

plain dresses were standing beside the front car looking down. On the ground and half under the car was their trouble shooter. He was checking a rear wheel.

The rear wheel was locked. Nothing could be done for it. The nearest mechanic was back in Hanksville, so the man in the sunglasses and his wife moved on in their car, with the Ohio plates, taking the driver of the disabled car along. The two women in the plain dresses got in with us.

They lived in Torrey, just beyond Capitol Reef, and that's where we were heading. They talked to us from the rear of the car. I was driving and I never knew for sure who was speaking. They said it was safe enough to go on, but I wasn't so sure myself. The sky was overcast. It looked like rain up ahead, and I was worried because of the deep, narrow passage through Capitol Reef.

"It's all right," one of them said. "You never get much rain this time of year." But I didn't think she sounded too sure of herself and I knew they were anxious to get on home. The last thing the Ohio couple had said before they drove off was, "Don't try to get through Capitol Reef's gorge if it even looks at all like rain." Then, at the entrance to the gorge, we saw a sign with the same stern warning.

"It's all right," a voice in the back said. "It's all right . . ." and we drove into a dry stream bed with steep, vertical banks of solid rock. The rain held off, but the going was slow. The road ran up, up; a steady incline, curving between high, massive stone banks. I kept listening, having heard enough stories of walls of water thundering down out of the mountains and through the arroyos around Santa Fe to make me uneasy now. The rain could be miles away, was what I'd heard: a cloudburst, a storm on the mountains' slopes was enough to get the torrent started.

I asked the women if they knew anyone who had ever been caught in where we were when it was running with water. "Oh yes . . ." It was when she was a child, said one, and traveling with her father. The flood had caught them, carrying their wagons away. They'd been stranded—almost died—and the road had been under twenty feet of water—but that was at a different time of year.

And then rain did begin to fall!

After a while, I switched on the windshield wiper. It was the rain that had followed us, doggedly, all the way across the country. "How much farther?" I asked. It was beginning to look as if that rain had got us just where it had wanted us all along.

She thought about another ten miles would get us out; and then, bless it, the rain slacked off. The road ran upward, damply but quietly. They were right enough about the season though, and we made it.

All their lives had been spent in this countryside. Brigham Young had sent their parents into the area as pioneers to establish a settlement that would be part of or perhaps even one more stake in the great tent that figuratively covered Deseret. In 1877, when Brigham Young died, there were more than 350 such stakes in that arid earth west of the prairies.

The woman talking didn't remember the marauding Indians herself, but her older sister had been killed by a party of Paiutes in 1879; and this was a state where Indian uprisings were not entirely things of the romantic past. Utah Indians had been on the warpath as late as 1921.

We cleared the gorge and drove on toward mountains that

the women called "hills." The one who had been caught in the flood said, "I was all over these hills as a girl. One of them is a dead volcano. I remember once we climbed its sides and looked in over the rim."

They got out at Torrey where the landscape was littered with black, volcanic stones, some of them as round as cannon shot.

The Mormon village we saw then at Torrey, and the ones we saw later along Frémont's old trail, now part of the length of Route 22, were unlike the larger Mormon towns. They were more like our early pioneer settlements: rustic, unpaved farm villages with unpainted frame and log houses set in among old cottonwood and cypress trees, the wood often weathered to a rich auburn. These were villages where cattle were still driven to and from the fields and up the village streets to their barns—and where the wagons that brought the hay in from the fields were pulled by horses.

It was haying time when we drove through Koosharem. The odor of the fresh-cut stems lay over the bare yards; and up along one of the village roads lay a trail of hay that had fallen from a wagon.

In Koosharem, a few buildings used brick, and the school was one. Here and there, the unpainted frame houses had windows trimmed in blue paint. In some of the yards around town, baled hay was piled in blocks twenty feet high. We drove back and forth through the streets: pole fences, homes with shingle roofs, plank fences. There was a stack of hay, a lighter yellow than the bales; and backyard gardens; and matted hay on the flat roof of a backyard shed.

Thirty-three miles to the south, there were barnyards in the town at Antimony as well—and one of the barnyards along the main street had a brook running through it with water as clear as a trout stream's. There's never an assortment of churches in these villages, as there are in so many small towns in the Middle West. There were a couple of Mormon churches in Antimony, but one was retired, no longer used as such. It was used for recreation. The boards by the front steps had been burned black from a fire that almost got out of hand. There was a constant danger of fire; and one of the buildings in town had burned so recently that it was still smoking the day we passed.

Near the scorched church was a monument on which a plaque had been placed by the Daughters of the Utah Pioneers: *PIONEERS OF ANTIMONY in 1873, Albert Goiser and others located in a fertile meadow which they named Grass Valley. Surveyors camped on a stream, lassoed a young coyote and called the place Coyote Creek. The first L.D.S. settlers were ISAAC RIDDLE and family who took up land on the east fork of the Sevier River. Later a school house was built, and the Marion Ward organized with Culbert King as Bishop. In 1920 the name was officially changed to Antimony after the antimony mines east of the valley.*

It was along this same stretch of back road in Utah that we passed what we thought at first was a cowboy. But he wasn't on his horse. He was on the ground, leaning against a telephone pole, staring around and taking it easy. He was herding sheep; and the sheep were just across the road.

Route 22 is a back road, a "lost" road and it leads past old Mormon mills, through a living pioneer era and past timeless Mormon villages. There was no ghostliness to any of them until we got to Grafton.

The sign to Grafton is a little to the west of Zion National Park at the edge of Route 15, and it points down a sandy road.

# THROUGH GIANT FOREST TO THE SEA

SEQUOIA NATIONAL FOREST, CALIFORNIA

"... a locomotive that was an old-timer pulled in ..."

"We put up one night beside a doctor and his wife who were out scouting for timeless towns."

NEAR FOUNTAIN SPRINGS, CALIFORNIA

"We passed cattle now, and . . . their ranges were these hills of hammered gold . . ."

SAN JUAN BAUTISTA, CALIFORNIA

"We came to San Juan Bautista."

SAN JUAN BAUTISTA, CALIFORNIA

"...museum pieces..."

SAN JUAN BAUTISTA, CALIFORNIA

"The hotel, next to the Breen house, was opened in 1858 and remained open until 1933."

SAN JUAN BAUTISTA, CALIFORNIA

"... the old poolroom and bar ..."

"... a never-never land on the wharf over the Pacific shore ..."

LAGUNITA, CALIFORNIA

"Some of the more recently built country schools are beginning to take on a timeless look . . ."

MONTEREY, CALIFORNIA

PT. LOBOS, CALIFORNIA

"... a sea that ran back into a white vapor out of which waves endlessly came ... and it was more like old Whitman facing west ... inquiring, tireless and seeking what was yet unfound."

The sand got deeper and deeper, and then it took digging and boards to get us back to the highway again. The road led nowhere. I'd walked on ahead of the car and the trail had petered out at the edge of a stream—without a road to be seen on the far side. Back on the highway, we drove a few hundred yards and parked. I'd seen a path.

We followed the path which led along a gully of brush and small trees; cut across a field; and came to a footbridge. It was an old bridge, its cables rusted and its boards sun-baked and broken; and it was a long bridge, too. It spanned the water to a small island where it anchored to a tree; and that was only half the trip. From the island, the bridge continued to a shore proper.

I went first. I inched along, testing each board. When I reached the island, I stopped and Mrs. H. started across. The cables swung and some of the footboards looked bad, but everything held together and, turn by turn, we made it to Grafton.

Beyond the narrow footbridge, we crossed a fenced-in field where cattle were grazing; and then, opening and closing a gate, we went down a long lane into a settlement of half a dozen substantial-looking houses. There was a church. Orchards were ripening. There was fresh hay in the loft of a barn. Except for a family at the end of town, no one lived in any of the houses, no one was moving about.

On our way back, the footbridge tilted and swayed. We worked our way along its rickety length, the sun hot on our heads and shoulders; and below us the stream sparkled.

I've heard it was the stream that finally cut the population of Grafton down and left its houses empty and its streets so ghostly. The town was too stranded from its source of supplies.

But here and there in the United States are splinter groups, outlawed by the main body of the Mormons, who want just that sort of isolation. Short Creek, Arizona, was such a place.

The law, of course, closed down on Short Creek. It's a ghost town of another kind. The Mormons put an end to "celestial marriage" in the last century, but it has a limited following, and a lot of parents in Short Creek are still in jail. They'll be back and the children are waiting.

Short Creek is just across the Arizona border along Route 59, a desert road. It was raining again when we pulled into town, and a big black milk cow was strolling up the middle of the road toward the general store and the post office. What few houses there were were scattered about with lots of space in between. There were a few unpainted frame houses and a couple of windmills on wooden towers.

As we left town, we drove by four kids who were wading, barefooted, in a puddle of rain water—something they rarely saw. The rain was falling and they had scarves tied over their heads. We waved to them, but they didn't, like most children might, wave back. They simply stood motionless and stared as we went by.

We swung on down to Pipe Spring National Monument which has an old Mormon stone fort that's been restored, and it's something of a museum now with its rooms furnished as they were in the last century. It's a desert oasis. In one of the buildings, we found a door typical of the region, decorated with nailheads that had rusted and run stains. The Mormons completed the fort in 1870. Later, it became a cattle ranch. A stream that once ran through the fort still runs through it today.

We went northward next, circling back—and then turned

west on Route 14 that took us over black volcanic fields past Cedar Breaks National Monument; down a white canyon to Cedar City; and out across desert.

We'd been traveling for forty-one days when we reached Modena, a few miles from the Nevada border. It's an old mining town with some buildings dating from around 1900—like the first store to appear in the settlement, which has a traditional square, fake front.

Following our road off to the southwest, we passed by the rock gorge that had some of the West's early freight haulers on the nervous edge of their wagon seats. And it wasn't holdup men that had them jumpy. There were some who said the gorge was haunted by the supernatural Gadianton Robbers. The Mormons knew all about them. They were a Satan-inspired band from among the aboriginal Americans: the Nephites and the Lamanites. But these particular Indians had little need for bows and arrows or the white man's rifle. They were perfectly capable of setting huge boulders in the path of the drivers—and of closing canyons upon them!

# 15

# ROADS WITHOUT
# TOWNS OR TRAFFIC

*Sundown at a line shack. Goldfield's waiting
gold. In the night at Death Valley. We cross
the Golden Hills.*

In the part of the West through which we were traveling
and along the roads we'd chosen, inns, as well as restaurants,
were as few and far between as most of the towns. But we'd
discovered the accommodations at the national monuments
and parks, and they make for interesting and reasonable overnight stops, although they're apt to be crowded in the summer.
It's well to be prepared to settle in at a campsite.

The parks preserve nature, and the nature they preserve is
impressive indeed. The buildings are designed to provide
maximum appreciation of the natural surroundings. This
means elaborate rustic style in such places as Bryce Canyon
National Park, where cabins with Indian rugs and stone fireplaces can be rented. Other parks we saw were Zion, Cedar
Breaks (off-trail, uncrowded, way up in the sky), and Capitol
Reef.

Lodge dinners, although overpriced, often afford spectacular views of wilderness solitude. But rolling along as we were, day by day, views nearly as spectacular were constantly with us, and anywhere we stopped to eat—there one was.

Moving into Nevada from Utah, the road crossed a series of mountain ridges and rolled over open, vacant rangeland. In Panaca, Nevada, we found a town with long sloping roofs that ran on down covering the front porch, the porch roofs supported by slim, square posts. There were shade trees and houses hidden in shade and foliage. And up a street came a boy mounted on the back of a big bay horse. He was riding barefooted and bareback, and a mongrel dog trotted along in the dust beside him.

At Caliente, the past was as good as salted away for keeps with yards and cottonwoods enclosed with picket fences; and the railroad station—built in the days and for the days when rail traffic was considerably heavier—looked like a Spanish mansion of stucco. This being Nevada, there was gambling. The gamblers' part of the picture, left over from the last century, can be found almost anywhere you care to look from the middle of town. On one side of the railroad tracks, we counted seven clubs and on the other, three.

Beyond town, in mountain desert scenery, we came across the first, for us, of the big pipe-organ cactus. It was forty-two miles to Hiko, and ahead were the mountains of the Pahranagat Range. It had been raining in Caliente and there was a haze in the air, the sky dark; almost no traffic. Over to our left, a slate-blue mist seemed to descend beyond the rim-rock into a bottomless abyss.

Hiko was still on our map as a town, but it was only a house with a post office. The buildings of the town were torn down and gone.

We drove past Hiko. The sides of the land to our right and left sloped up into mountain crags and rocks as smoothly as swelling sea at land's edge, flowing up in among the ridges. It was after Hiko that we hit a stretch of paved road that ran for over one hundred miles through uninhabited desert.

After some fifty miles we saw at last a small log house, a pond, and a windmill far back at the end of a narrow driveway. It looked as if there might be a lake to the west of the line shack, but from our distance it was hard to tell. There were cattle about and some were over by the lake or the salt flat, whichever it was. The shack looked uninhabited and deserted. We turned down the long driveway to go see; and it was. The wind was blowing. I pulled in close to the house, beside the front door that faced the highway. Evening was close at hand and the time had come to eat. Mrs. H. went off to investigate the lake, but it was a lonely, desolate countryside and she didn't go far. She came back shortly. I had taken the gasoline stove into the shack and set it up on a wooden table. Everything was covered with an alkali dust. I spread newspapers. The window glass in the east wall was filmed with dust, too, and had bullet holes in it. There were two rooms to the shack, the main room of logs in which I was, and a smaller room with walls insulated by cardboard cartons that had been nailed to the wood planks on all four sides.

We ate in the car as the sun went down; and the show the mountains and the clouds and the sun put on that evening was the most extravagantly colorful one of the whole trip. Out on the highway, no cars went past; there might as well not have been a highway—or for that matter, no cars yet invented.

In the night, before I slept, I began to think about the

176

Johnson boys, Carl and Bob, though why I don't know. I was thinking back to my high school days, to that time when the Belt Line's concrete was being poured across the eastern countryside of Grand Rapids, Michigan. I lay in the cab darkness, looking up and out through the door in the roof that framed a piece of the sky. I was thinking of the house where they'd lived. I could remember the wallpaper, and I could see the upright piano that I used to sit down at as soon as I came in. I'd sit down and bang out the Eddy Duchin theme, the only thing besides "Chopsticks" I'd ever learned.

I suppose I was remembering back to a time I'd been thoroughly carefree. That must have been it, because I felt the loss of time as I lay there, seeing little corners of that period so vividly that I was half there again and half where I lay looking up at the night.

I lost track of the Johnsons after the war. They all moved out of the state and west to . . . I couldn't remember. I thought it was Iowa: maybe Cedar Rapids, maybe it was Des Moines.

In Tama, I thought about checking through the telephone directories for those cities, looking for their names among the many Johnsons, but I didn't. Mrs. H. had said, "Why don't you?" And I'd said, "I don't know . . . what would I say? All I could do would be to sing our old high school song."

"How does that go?"

I sang a little: "Comstock Park, we're for youuuu; Comstock Park, we're true blueee . . ."

"That's enough," she said.

"That's all I remember."

"It's just as well."

And that was about the way I felt. What I saw as I lay there were the faces of a couple of kids that could have been, in age, sons of mine if I'd got started on a family as young as some of my friends of those days had; but I felt no older than that myself as I lay there wondering what had happened to them. This is one of the tricks of the mind that makes it willing to believe the past does live on somehow or other at the end of some lost road, weed-grown and leaf-drifted.

The next morning along the rest of that stretch of road to Warm Springs, we met only one car; and we passed only one building. We rolled across treeless desert, through unfenced range where only a few forlorn steers were wandering their purgatory in a perfect desert daze.

A few miles from Warm Springs, which had been an old coach stop, there was a cluster of houses. Then it was another similar 52 miles to Tonopah, Nevada, one of the famous old silver queens of the West. Its mines were no longer rumbling, but this was a region out of which half a billion dollars in ore had come.

We turned south on 95 for Goldfield—moving off toward Death Valley and California.

Up until 1902, Goldfield has been known as Grandpa, and then a little more than fifty years after the hills of California began to echo with the sounds of picks, folks discovered that Grandpa was a virtual field of gold. The town's name was fittingly changed to something that better conveyed the fabulousness of rock worth up to $50 and even $100 a pound. One pile of ore, weighing 47 tons, was worth better than half a million dollars. Miners swarmed in and the population boomed; reached 30,000 in the early part of this century. But miners working for mineowners began to pocket a little of this high-grade ore. Because of the strikes and riots that followed this "high-grading," the state police were needed to keep law and order.

Although we found Goldfield still an inhabited town, time, nevertheless, had hung up his scythe back about 1923, the town's last "good" year . . . and the atmosphere was even older. Most of the houses dated back to the beginning years of the century, when the boom started and the town got big and important enough for Joe Gans and Battling Nelson to fight their famous endurance brawl of 42 rounds on September 3, 1906.

Tex Ricard's old saloon has burned, and Pete Moser has a gas station on the site now. Fire hit a lot of the town in 1923, gutted the walls of an old saloon and gambling hall near the local school. While we were sitting looking at it, a couple of men with shovels came walking up the street toward us. They were both lean men in Western blue denim. They hadn't shaved in a day or so, and they were striding along as though they knew where they were going and there was no time to waste. As they came by, one of them looked over at us and grinned. "If you hear us yell," he said, "you'll know we struck it rich." And they went on down the street and turned at the road that went past a house whose Bible-quoting owner had painted with THOU SHALT NOT STEAL and had then locked up and left, to return to in better days. They went past the house and headed steadily down the road out of town, the silvery, spade-heads of their shovels bobbing behind them.

Whether they were after gold or not, I don't know. Most of the people around town seemed to be waiting for the price of gold to go up before they started digging again.

At the Santa Fe Club, where I went for a drink of something cool, a powerful man, hair gone gray, cigar in his teeth, stood behind the bar and spoke of the price of gold. It was a dusky place. The fixtures dated back to the year 1905 and quiet rested on all of them like a dusty film of the past.

The bartender was the owner, and he had mine property around Goldfield. It was full of low-grade ore that would be valuable once the price of gold went up—and he was expecting it to go up almost any day. Long overdue, he said. He was waiting. He was waiting in a cave of time, and I had the feeling that all the old objects might then reawaken to the same life they'd once known if the price of gold ever did go up: the way the toys in the toymaker's workshop awaken at a magical midnight moment that lasts until a mortal dawn.

Half the homes in Goldfield were vacant, boarded-up, or the windows broken. The town's hotel, a four-story, red-brick building was closed. But there were a few people around. Men were walking along the streets, and dogs were ambling about here and there. The Santa Fe Club was still doing business, and its customers still had a wooden sidewalk to use to reach it, as well as unpaved streets. It was still like the old days, though things had come down a little, gotten worn and sometimes broken. Outside the bar, on the porch, the backs and the seats of wooden chairs, having lost their legs, were nailed to the tops of wooden crates. But things were getting broken and worn fifty years ago, too.

That same afternoon, we reached California by way of Death Valley. We rolled down the sloping sides of the road into Death Valley and into a nacreous mist . . . or was it steam?

About five miles from where the road turned to lead away straight and far back into the valley, we caught sight of sand

dunes. They were over to our right and at or near the foot of
the far mountains. They were the first acres of sand we'd seen
along the way; and since I'd once imagined the whole West
to be a sandpile with endless edges, the sight of the dunes
was like a mission of the imagination accomplished; now I'd
finally seen the West.

It was six o'clock and a milky white heat lay all about us.
We were submerged in it. There wasn't an animal or a bird
to be seen until we got to the National Monument Headquarters and there, on the grass which must be constantly
watered, were a pair of jackrabbits, back to back, nibbling the
lawn and keeping it as well-trimmed as honed and spinning
blades. There wasn't any need to fence them in to keep them
at work—where else, being in Death Valley, could they go?
The lawn was in excellent shape and they'd become fairly
tame: intrepid mowers in a sea of heat.

Furnace Creek Inn was closed for the summer. It's a chunk
of de luxe hotel security among date palms in the midst of
that sand. We'd have gone on but I'd heard how deserts cool
off at night. I can only say now that a strong breeze blew.

That night, the breeze that blew came at us as if forced
from gigantic fans far up the valley, and it was oven-fresh
. . . and so were we in short order. Sleep was impossible.
Some time after midnight we drove back to pick up Route 190
and we stopped at the National Monument Headquarters
to fill our vacuum bottles with ice-cold water from the cooler
in the lobby, and to drink and drink and drink. The rabbits
were still at it out on the lawn. It took us about twenty miles
to rise 5000 feet; and at Townes Pass we got some sleep.

The next morning there were jagged summits on our left
and black and green hills to our right. I saw Frémont moving

against them, and he was a young man. It was like the night I'd thought of the Johnson boys and saw them not the age they are now, but still the age I last saw and recalled them. I saw Frémont as a young man and I saw myself, so many years before I would be born, a young man standing not only among the same summits but in the same age that was Frémont's. In the mind, at least, all time can exist simultaneously.

It's in the mind that time is anachronistic through and through. In my fancy, I stood once, for instance, in a Western saloon, elbow to elbow with a knight in armor as we drank and gazed behind the bar at a picture of Joe Louis with his gloves on. And that's the way the trip had been. And that's the way the trip had gone. That morning, our forty-third, only two nights were between us and the Pacific. The trip was nearly done.

We descended a narrow road, a winding slot in the mountains—down into another valley, the Panamint; and up the valley floor ran a river of pure sand. We crossed it on highway, as if the river of sand, like the Jordan, had parted for us. Lizards arched their tails and skittered as we came down the road, and by the side of the road lay charcoal black, time-licked stones.

Keeler, California, was a timeless town, a town cut off by a new highway. There were no sidewalks; and while we were there, a locomotive that was an old-timer pulled in, Number 9 of the Southern Pacific.

At Lone Pine, we turned south and made our way along the edge of the ridge of mountains toward Walker Pass. Then turning west on 178, there were joshua trees on each side of us; and beyond the pass we picked up the Kern River; and then went down, down into a green valley; then up again into the Greenhorn Mountains—and beyond the mountains, the smooth, yellow hills of California appeared. They lay ahead of us, fold upon yellow fold, with pockets of deep shadow. The hills were set with clusters of gray boulders, and brown fence posts were strung tightly with barbed wire. We passed cattle now, and sometimes they were in corrals beside the road. Their ranges were these hills of hammered gold . . . and these were the hills, this was the land that had pulled the population of the East across the prairies beginning with the Bidwell-Bartleson Company's immigration train of 1841.

That was well before the gold rush period beginning in '49. The gold rush didn't last so long, about five years; and California went right on pulling the pioneers West. In 1850, with the help of the present state's gold, the population topped 92,000. Ten years later, it was approaching 400,000. And that was still in the stagecoach days. The transcontinental railroad was completed in 1869, and the Westward roll of the settlers was really under way. The stagecoaches were finished, but they didn't know it yet.

In 1877, the Omaha *Herald* printed the following list of travel tips for stagecoach passengers:

"The best seat inside a stage is the one next to the driver. Even if you have a tendency to seasickness when riding backwards, you'll get over it and will get less jolts and jostling. Don't let any sly elph trade you his midseat.

"In cold weather don't ride with tight fitting boots, shoes or gloves. When the driver asks you to get off and walk, do so without grumbling. He won't request it unless absolutely necessary. If the team runs away—sit still and take your chances. If you jump; nine out of ten times you will get hurt.

183

"In very cold weather abstain entirely from liquor when on the road; because you will freeze twice as quickly when under its influence.

"Don't growl at the food received at the station; stage companies generally provide the best they can get. Don't keep the stage waiting. Don't smoke a strong pipe inside the coach—spit on the leeward side. If you have anything to drink in a bottle pass it around. Procure your stimulants before starting as 'ranch' (stage depot) whiskey is not 'nectar.'

"Don't swear or lop over neighbors when sleeping. Take small change to pay expenses. Never shoot on the road as the noise might frighten the horses. Don't discuss politics or religion. Don't point out where murders have been committed if there are women passengers.

"Don't lag at the wash basin. Don't grease your hair because travel is dusty. Don't imagine for a moment that you are going on a picnic. Expect annoyances, discomfort, and some hardship."

Nevertheless, when the transcontinental railroad line was completed 290 years after Sir Francis Drake, sailing the *Golden Hind* dropped anchor in a California bay, the stagecoach and the river boats and the canal boats were done for. Today (history moving along at a faster rate of change than ever, and the American population still on the move), it's the passenger railroads that appear to be losing ground as the automobiles increase—and toll roads, too.

In Taos, New Mexico, the Indians, who seem to have held their own for several centuries, are feeling surly about a highway some of the local businessmen want to run across their reservation. Rural schools are getting fewer and fewer: in

Tama County, Iowa, there are now only twenty-three where there were 103 in 1945. Covered bridges and river ferries are vanishing. The summer before last, on the Ohio, the last of the river's showboats was up for sale. Tractors have, as every school child knows, replaced the farm horse. Old Dobbin is gone. Towns are disappearing. Imagine how a man must feel returning home to the vista of his boyhood in Dawson, New Mexico. It's gone—once a town of 7000; the mines and homes dismantled and the ground plowed over. He'd stand among grazing cattle on what used to be main street.

I doubt, at that, if his dismay would be any greater than the man felt who returned to Wichita, Kansas, after being away for twenty-five years. He hadn't seen it since the Depression, back about the time I watched the Belt Line built past my grandmother's house—and he wandered the streets and gazed about in amazement. He couldn't spot a thing he recognized. There was nothing left, not a building he remembered, until he came upon the Masonic Home, he said, at Seneca and Maple.

Along the highways now, instead of at the river banks or beside the tracks of a railroad, towns are growing—spreading, merging. The strip cities are taking shape. But wait—mysteriously, something of all this past of ours does remain. It's caught here and there in pockets and valleys of time, virtually unchanged. It's all out there in that vast area round the cities that stretch along the big highways. All we had to do, I knew, was turn off the highways to find it. It was there. Others are beginning to find it too.

We put up one night beside a doctor and his wife who were out scouting for timeless towns. People all over the country seem to be of a mind to turn back down the quiet uncrowded roads to covered stairways and town pumps and land unsettled and uninhabited as far as one can see in any direction.

On the morning of our forty-fourth day west, we drove through the Sequoia National Forest. We drove among trees that live longer and grow larger than anything on earth. Most of those trees had been alive before the timeless towns we'd seen had even been built—before lost roads—before there'd been a United States of America.

From the park, we turned west again, driving down the mountainside along a narrow road numbered 65, and there were brown earth embankments on our left where the roots of trees had broken loose and were bare to the sunlight. The leaves of the live oak trees had already turned to burned fall browns . . . because, we heard, of the drought.

Beyond Auckland, turning more directly west along Route 63, suddenly, a fertile valley at the bottom of an incline and the shiny green patina of orchards. We followed a dirt road. Near Dinuba (echoes of Steinbeck) a bus was loading up with Mexican fruit-pickers. It was then 5 P.M.

The land became as flat as Kansas. The fruit orchards were gone. There were irrigation canals all around.

We had dinner in Dos Palos at Santi's Restaurant. It was an attractive place and the chef whose name was Sal had a special on beef Stroganoff. It cost $2.75 and that included shrimp cocktail, salad, and dessert. A double martini was 85 cents.

On the morning of our last day West, we left Dos Palos and crossed the San Joaquin Valley toward the Diablo Range. About twenty miles from the Pacific Ocean and about ten from Salinas, we came to San Juan Bautista.

The Spanish founded a mission here in 1797. It was along

their Camino Real. The buildings around the plaza haven't changed much since the place was used for bullfights, and California still belonged to Spain. Mexico took over in 1820 and held on for about twenty years, and then the town became part of the United States.

The American period began after the Breen family arrived. They had just survived, as members of the Donner party, one of the most macabre pioneer disasters in our history.

The hotel, next to the Breen house, was opened in 1858 and remained open until 1933. It's now a museum with the old poolroom and bar, as well as a number of other rooms, preserved as they were. Several buildings around the plaza house museum pieces, as does a yard that's filled with old wagons.

Aside from the plaza, which is now a national monument, the town made up of the surrounding streets is also tucked away in a fold of the past. It's not quite so old as Spanish colonial days, but it dates to a pleasant and earlier period of California's, to a time around the opening of the century.

Even buildings that go back only twenty years or less, like some of the more recently built country schools, are beginning to take on a "timeless" look these days; and there's a rural school looking ageless along the road between San Juan Bautista and Salinas on the Salinas Road. They're disappearing as the school buses make the long haul from countryside to town.

Moving along the Carmel Valley, we reached the Pacific at Point Lobos; behind us were a long trail of lost towns and more than a few of the country's lost roads. Though there was a mist on the sea, as there'd been out over the Atlantic on our first morning of the trip, the Pacific was a different-looking ocean.

The waves came in as endlessly, but they were bigger and wondrously sedate. They hove in out of the mist and broke their serenity against the rocks and cliffs along the shore.

We parked and got out and took a path that led up among the Monterey cypress. I remembered something.

"What's the matter?"

"You go on," I said. "There's something I forgot."

I turned and went back down the path at a trot. When I reached the car, I unlocked the back, raised it—then opened the cabinet doors and felt around. I took out all the cans and bottles and boxes. I even lifted the shelf paper and looked under it. But it was nowhere.

I headed back up the path again, slowly. Not far beyond where I'd told Mrs. H. to go ahead, the path forked. I stopped. The path to the left led more directly to the cliffs and the sea, and I took that one.

The cypress trees were wind-twisted, the limbs all bewitched. It was a lonely little area of shaded fantasia, and there were ropes on each side of the path. I came out in an open place and there below was the sea. From out of the mist to the west, big waves were rolling into shore, smashing into the rocks down below. Out on the water, a rocky island was dark with birds and seals.

Mrs. H. was nowhere in sight. We'd taken separate paths at the fork; I'd guessed wrong and I missed her now. But as though all paths join anyway, she came down the path toward me from the other direction, the wind blowing her hair. She was grinning.

"Is this," she said, "what you wanted?"

I checked the stone to be sure it was the same one. "I figured you were guarding this."

188

"I was; but if it means something to you, heave away."

Faced with the vastness of a sea that ran back into a white vapor out of which waves endlessly came toward shore, the gesture wasn't the grand finale I'd thought it was going to be. She was right—as if endings as well as beginnings can't be made but are best found in memory. The stone arced out and it was a small moving point against the sky and then against the mist and then it dropped through the white-flecked blue without a ripple to leave behind. Nature and Time combined to overwhelm the gesture; and it was more like old Whitman facing west from California's shore: inquiring, tireless and seeking what was yet unfound. So this is not an ending. There isn't any, for trips through time.

We drove then along the ocean to Monterey. It was the fifth of August and it was about 2:30 in the afternoon. We'd come 7484 miles in 45 days. We took the Seventeen Mile Drive. So much of the "lost land" is back where our grand-fathers and our great-grandfathers stand in shadow, but there are roads that lead there. The roads also lead to places only the imagination knows, raised for us out of fiction and the silver screen of a dark movie house—like the West I once pictured as all rippled sand dunes with cowboys in buckskin slung with pearl-handled six-shooters; or even like that never-never land on the wharf over the Pacific shore with the fishing boats at anchor at Monterey.

# INDEX

# Index

# Index

Pennsylvania, towns in: Bedford, 67; Big Broad Top, 66; Connellsville, 69; Doylestown, 46; East Berlin, 61; East Petersburg, 59; Gettysburg, 59–63; Glen Savage, 68; Greencastle, 64; Harleysville, 47; Hyndman, 68; Manheim, 59; Mercersburg, 65; Mont Alto, 63; New Britain, 46; New Salem, 70; Pughtown, 48; Robertsdale, 66; Royersford, 48; Saxton, 67; Schwenksville, 47; Shadygrove, 64; Spring City, 48; Warwick, 48; Waynesboro, 63–64; York, 60–61

Putnam, Gen. Rufus, 90

Rapp, Rev. George, 104
Ricard, Tex, 179
River boats, 93–94; Delta Queen, 103
Road building, 92–94, 116
Roads, early: Camino Real, 187; Chisholm Trail, 128; Forbes Road, 67; Frémont's Trail, 169; Michigan Road, 99, 101; Natchez Trace, 99; National Road, 93, 101; Santa Fe Trail, 127, 130, 138, 142, 144; Spanish Trail, 160; Wilderness Road, 99; Zane's Trace, 93, 99
Robber's Roost Gang, 166

Sherman, Able, 91–92, 115
Snake fence, 156
South, timeless places in the: Mobile, Ala., 25; Memphis, Tenn., 26; Greenville, Memphis, Natchez, Vicksburg, Miss., 26; Lafayette, Natchitoches, Bayou La Fourche, New Orleans, La., 26; Charleston, S.C., 26; Savannah, Ga., 26; Great Smoky Mountains, 26; Shenandoah Valley, 26; Lexington, Mount Vernon, Va., 27

Stage coach travelers' tips, 183
State guides, 21

Taos Indians, 142–43
Texas, timeless places in: Big Bend National Park, 28; San Antonio, 28
Thirteen Colonies, 23
Twain, Mark, 16

Uncle Tom's Cabin, 100
Uncompahgre National Forest, 156
Utah, Bryce Canyon National Park, 174
Utah, Capitol Reef National Monument, 166–68, 174
Utah, Cedar Breaks National Monument, 173, 174
Utah, Dead Horse Point, 159
Utah, hotels and/or restaurants in: see National Parks, 174
Utah, Natural Bridges National Monument, 160
Utah, towns in: Antimony, 169–70; Blanding, 160; Cedar City, 173; Fruita, 160; Grafton, 170–71; Hanksville, 165–68; Hite, 161–63; Hys Bottom, 159; Koosharem, 169; Moab, 158; Modena, 173; Torrey, 167, 169; White Canyon, 161
Utah, Zion National Park, 170, 174

Village life, early, Middle West, 116–18, 126–27
Virginia, Williamsburg, 21

Wells, H. G., 77
West Virginia, 85
Whitman, Walt, 29, 62, 189
Wisconsin, 28
Woods, John, 95, 100, 102, 104, 106, 107
Wyoming, Jackson Hole, 28

Young, Brigham, 168

194

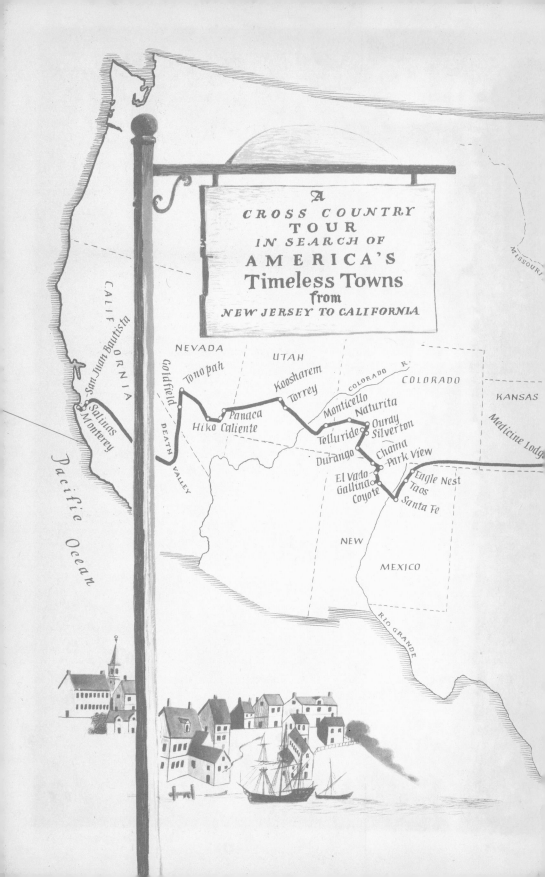

A CROSS COUNTRY TOUR IN SEARCH OF AMERICA'S Timeless Towns from NEW JERSEY TO CALIFORNIA